NAMESAKES

NAMESAKES

An Entertaining Guide to the Origins of More Than 300 Words Named for People

TAD TULEJA

A STONESONG PRESS BOOK

McGraw-Hill Book Company

New York St. Louis San Francisco Auckland Bogotá
Hamburg Johannesburg London Madrid Milan Mexico
Montreal New Delhi Panama Paris São Paulo Singapore
Sydney Tokyo Toronto

For my family:

Andrée, Noah, Adriana, and India

First McGraw-Hill Paperback edition, 1987

1 2 3 4 5 6 7 8 9 FGRFGR 8 7

ISBN 0-07-065436-0

LIBRARY OF CONGRESS CATALOGING-IN-PUBLICATION DATA

Tuleja, Tad, 1944–
Namesakes.
Bibliography: p.
Includes index.
1. English language—Eponyms—Dictionaries.
I. Title.
PE1583.T85 1987 423'.1 86-15216
ISBN 0-07-065436-0

BOOK DESIGN BY KATHRYN PARISE

Contents

Contents

Introduction

"Why do they call it a Ferris wheel?"

This question was put to me by my twelve-year-old as we swayed high above the cotton candy stands at a recent summer carnival. I gave it two seconds' thought. "It was invented by a guy named Ferris."

"Amazing, Dad. What was his first name? Did he work in a carnival? What did he—"

"Eat your cotton candy," I advised. "When we get home you can look it up."

"You always say that," he grumbled. I had been pitching him this Stengelism lately—Casey was fond of capping his baseball stories with the tag line "You could look it up"—and he had begun to resent it. What he didn't know was that, in this particular case, I had no choice. For all I knew, Ferris was an acronym or somebody's pet piranha.

When we got home we took Casey's advice and looked it up. Ferris was an engineer, which we agreed was a good thing. A very American engineer, having been christened George Washington Gale Ferris. He lived at the turn of the century and designed his famous midway attraction for the 1893 Columbian Exposition. No indication in the source books if he got rich off the deal or worked as a barker on the side.

So far, so good—but then the rub. As soon as we had disinterred old G.W.G.F. from a century of neglect, I began to hear voices. Sometimes proud, sometimes indignant, often plaintive. "You got Ferris straight," they said. "What about us?"

The voices had names and claims. Achilles' heel and the Doppler effect. Pollyanna and the Rube Goldberg contraption. The Geiger counter and chicken à la king. Who were these forgotten souls who had lent their names to principles and inventions and carnival attractions—and now were vying for the title of Most Obscure Hero with St. Aloysius and Millard Fillmore?

Consider the casual, nay cavalier, attitude that most of us have toward these folks. How many times have you referred to some potential, brooding disaster as a "sword of Damocles" without wondering who Damocles was? How often have you read a thermometer without giving a thought to Daniel Fahrenheit or Anders Celsius? Are hookers really named for Joseph Hooker? And who was Tom Collins, anyway?

It was to answer questions of this order that I put together the volume in your hands. Terms named for people are called eponyms, from the Greek *onyma,* for "name." *Namesakes* is a dictionary of such terms.

"Term" of course is imprecise, but that is inevitable given the ubiquity of eponymous influence. An eponym may refer to a physical principle (Doppler effect), a food (fettuccine Alfredo), an exclamation of surprise (by Jove), or a philosophical guideline (Occam's razor). It may be an obvious namesake such as the foregoing examples, or a subtler, "hidden" namesake such as saxophone, protean, or Frisbee. The *onyma* being invoked may be that of an actual person (Bloody Mary or Joseph Pulitzer), a mythical being (Mercury of the mercurial temper, Achilles of the vulnerable heel), or a fictional creation (Pollyanna or Scrooge). The source may be relatively obvious, as in Bowie knife and Nehru jacket; or relatively obscure, as in derrick, sideburns, and nerd.

Because of the range of eponyms in our language, the writer setting out to compile a list of possible entries is struck first by the latitude, and then by the vanity, of the task. To put together a "complete" list of such terms, you quickly discover, is about as viable a job, to quote Ring Lardner from another context, as "catching whales with an angleworm." In my original design for this book, I came up with something like 1,500 "possibles." Since I had not yet invented the thirty-two-hour day, and since I wanted *Namesakes* to appeal to the generally educated reader, not the pedant, it was clearly time to trim sail.

In getting the original list down to the slightly more than 300 entries you have here, I had to play Procrustes three times.

First, I weeded out all but the most common eponymous terms from the specialized vocabulary of the sciences. This meant that, with great reluctance, I had to bid adieu to such tasty morphological morsels as Fibonacci series and Chandrasekhar limit, islets of Langerhans and Boyle's law. To science-minded readers who wish the basic dope on such terms, I recommend Denis Ballentyne and D. R. Lovett's exhaustive *Dictionary of Named Effects*.

Second, I wiped out the history. This was hard going but inevitable, for if you held on to Braddock's defeat, pretty soon you had Hannibal's march and Custer's last stand and a Fibonacci series of minor battles. So it was goodbye to Shays's rebellion, Beecher's Bibles, and (my most sorely missed gobbet) the world-shattering War of Jenkins's Ear. I apologize to my fellow Cliophiles, and especially to my father and father-in-law, both historians, for this unwelcome necessity.

Finally, I said goodbye to those entries that were linguistically simply too archaic to mean much to a modern audience. In another incarnation, perhaps, I shall restore to their proper place in the word-hoard such once common expressions as Piso's justice, Fred Karno's army, and phaeton. *Namesakes* was not the place to do this.

What is left after this triple excision is, I trust, a moderately comprehensive, educational, and entertaining guide to terms that you hear, if not every day, at least once or twice a year; that derive from proper names; and whose eponymous owners have, in many cases, been unfairly forgotten by history. I will think of my time as well spent if *Namesakes* allows readers to distinguish between Niccolò Machiavelli, John Mack, and Ernst Mach; or to win bar bets on the dates of William Spooner.

With a few exceptions, the entries are arranged alphabetically. Interspersed throughout the text are a number of noneponymous subheadings under which I have arranged related namesakes that did not lend themselves to fuller treatment: for example, Caesar salad, Windsor knot, and Peeping Tom. These subheadings appear at the end of their alphabetical categories.

At the end of the book you will find two further sections:

"Collective Eponyms" and "False Leads." These contain entries that do not derive, strictly speaking, from personal names, but that are still relevant, and often fascinating, to the eponymologist: for example, the collective namesakes Spartan and thug; and the false leads tin Lizzie and blanket.

SMALL CAPITALS throughout refer to the text entries listed in the Index.

My indebtedness to printed sources is indicated in the Bibliography. My thanks also to Paul Fargis of the Stonesong Press, who squired the idea into a contract; Dr. Marios Philippides, who gave me advice on the classical entries; and the numerous friends and family members who helped to unstick my linguistic gears.

T. F. T.

Belchertown, Mass.
1987

NAMESAKES

A

Achilles' Heel

The fiercest and most famous of the Greek heroes, Achilles is the tragic protagonist of Homer's *Iliad*. The unifying theme of that long MARTIAL epic is the anger of Achilles at being deprived of his favorite slave girl, Briseis, by the Greek commander Agamemnon in the final year of the Trojan War. Homer describes Achilles' refusal to fight with his fellow Greeks after the appropriation of the girl; the onslaught of the Trojans against the Greeks, now missing their most valiant warrior; Hector's killing of Achilles' friend Patroclus, who, dressed in the sulking hero's armor, had rallied the Greeks; and Achilles' return to the fray to avenge Patroclus by killing Hector. Homer hints at, but does not describe, the subsequent death of Achilles at the hand of Paris; according to several ancient traditions, Paris succeeded where all others had failed by shooting an arrow into the Greek's one vulnerable spot, his heel. Hence our terms *Achilles' heel* for an analogous point of weakness and *Achilles tendon* for the tendon between the heel and the calf.

The petulant hero survived as long as he did because of a canny mother, the sea nymph Thetis. At his birth, according to a popular legend, she had dipped him into the underworld river Styx, whose waters had made him invincible—except at the spot where she held him, by the heel. No one has ever satisfactorily explained this oversight in her foresight.

Adonis

Like NARCISSUS and HYACINTH, Adonis was a handsome Greek youth whose tragic death is remembered by a flower—in his case the anemone. His name now means any handsome male.

Adonis figures prominently in James Frazer's *The Golden Bough,* which makes it clear that he was imported from Babylonia. In Babylonia he was known as Tammuz, the lover of the mother goddess Ishtar; as a personification of the seasonal cycle, he spends half the year above ground with her, the other half in the underworld with Ishtar's infernal counterpart, Allatu. The Semitic term *adon* means "lord," and it was as Adon Tammuz, and ultimately just as Adon, that he became known to the Greeks.

In Greece Adonis is the beloved of Aphrodite, goddess of love, who gives him to Persephone for safekeeping when he is still a child. Persephone, the daughter of Demeter and the unwilling bride of Hades, falls for him too, and will not surrender him to Aphrodite until Zeus decrees that Adonis shall spend half his year above ground and half below. Thus he becomes, like Tammuz and like Persephone herself, a mythic embodiment of death and rebirth. The terrestrial evidence of his death is the bright red windflower, or anemone, which blooms brilliantly for a very short time. The Greeks say it blooms from his blood, shed from the fatal goring he received on the horns of a fierce wild boar. Others contend it was Mars, jealous of Aphrodite's love for him, who assumed the beast's shape and ran him through.

Aesop's Fables

It is not known where or when Aesop lived, or indeed if he lived at all. Ancient traditions call him a slave from Phrygia the country of Gordius (see GORDIAN KNOT) and Midas (see MIDAS TOUCH), say he lived in the sixth century B.C., and often portray him as deformed; there is also some agreement that he died at the hands of a Delphian mob whose famous oracle he had insulted. But whether he was legend or fact, centuries of readers have appreciated the animal tales attributed to him.

Aesop's fables include such classics of folklore as the story of the fox and the (sour) grapes and that of the tortoise and the hare. They were first written down in the first century A.D., by the rather pedestrian Roman author Phaedrus. His Latin version formed the basis for subsequent medieval tellings, and for those of La Fontaine. The tag lines or "morals" of the stories, considered so characteristic of Aesop, were probably added much later: the first popular English edition of the tales, the 1722 version by Samuel Croxall, with its series of social and political "applications," helped to make this aspect of "Aesop" widely known.

Aesopian is now frequently applied to any anecdote in which animals exemplify human traits. The adjective, like the title *Aesop's Fables* itself, is a misnomer, since some of his eponymous tales are depicted on Egyptian papyri dating from a thousand years before his time.

Horatio Alger Story

One of the most cherished of American myths is that of the self-made man: the idea that with enough determination and grit anyone can rise from poverty to prominence. Horatio Alger, whose name is synonymous with "rags to riches," probably did more to sustain this myth than Abraham Lincoln and Andrew Carnegie combined.

Born in Massachusetts, Alger (1834–99) was the son of a Unitarian minister and apparently inherited some of his father's sanctimoniousness: he was known among schoolmates as "Holy Horatio." Graduated from Harvard Divinity School in 1860, he became a Unitarian minister himself four years later, but in 1866 he resigned and moved to New York City to devote himself to writing. There he became associated with the Newsboys' Lodging House, a street urchins' shelter whose inhabitants provided him with much material for his fiction.

His first literary success came with the story "Ragged Dick," serialized in 1867. It was followed by a string of *Ragged Dick* novels which set the pattern for all of Alger's work: an industrious working-class youth wins both the girl and his fortune by devotion to moral principles and hard work. This pattern worked its way through 119 books, including the bestselling series *Luck and Pluck*

(1869) and *Tattered Tom* (1871), and several uplifting biographies including *Abraham Lincoln the Backwoods Boy* (1883). Between the Gilded Age and the Roaring Twenties—when Alger's work enjoyed a revival—an estimated 20 million copies of his books were sold.

In spite of (or because of) his characters' simpleminded probity, Alger exerted a tremendous influence on nineteenth-century social ideals. Careful readers have pointed out that luck generally has as much to do with the typical Alger hero's success as does effort; and that the success is always quite modest (the Bible-bred author was keenly aware of the moral hazards of riches). Such subtleties were lost on most readers, however, and for generations of would-be millionaires, the Horatio Alger success story—with the gray areas conveniently forgotten—served as a set piece of the American dream.

Ampere

The standard unit of electrical current is the *ampere* (in electrician's jargon, the *amp*), commonly defined as the current produced by one VOLT applied against a one-OHM resistance. It was named for French physicist André Marie Ampère (1775–1836), whose work on the relationship between electricity and magnetism laid the foundations of modern electrodynamics.

Born into a wealthy merchant's family in Lyon, Ampère educated himself in the family library, lost his father to the GUILLOTINE in 1793, and after the Revolution began a teaching career, first in central France and after 1804 in Paris. Although elected to the Academy of Sciences in 1814, he did not conduct his most significant scientific work until the 1820s, when he demonstrated that an electrical current could excite a magnetic field and shift it in the direction of the current flow. He gave his name not only to the ampere but to *Ampère's theorem,* which defines the relationship between electrical and magnetic force; and to *Ampère's law,* which quantifies the interactive force between nearby current-carrying wires.

Aphrodisiac

Love potions are called *aphrodisiacs* after the Greek goddess of beauty and love, Aphrodite. Her name recalls her curious origin. As the eighth-century poet Hesiod tells the tale, when the Titan (see TITANIC) leader Cronus overthrew his father, the original sky god Uranus, he castrated him and threw his genitals into the sea; out of the *aphros* that formed around them, the beautiful goddess was born. Since *aphros* means both "foam" and "semen," her name is a double entendre, meaning both "foam born" and "semen born." The Romans knew Aphrodite as Venus, and Botticelli's famous painting *The Birth of Venus,* jokingly called "Venus on the Half Shell," is a representation of this myth.

As befitted the patroness of sexual desire, Aphrodite had many lovers. Zeus gave her in marriage to Hephaestus (see VOLCANO), and her frequent trysts with the war god Ares (see MARTIAL) made Hephaestus a prototype of the cuckold. Her children by Ares were Phobos (Fear), from which we get *phobia;* Harmonia (Concord), from which *harmony;* and Deimos (Terror). With Hermes she produced Hermaphrodite, a child with both male and female characteristics who gives us our word *hermaphrodite*. With Dionysus (see DIONYSIAN) she bore the god Priapus, a faunlike creature whom Zeus's wife, Hera, jealous of Aphrodite's amours, endowed with a constant erection; hence our term *priapic,* for "phallic."

As Venus, of course, the love goddess has had a higher profile than Aphrodite. From the Middle Ages on, she has been the embodiment of physical perfection and carnal love—to which painters since the Renaissance have testified. The adjective *venereal* comes from her name.

Arachnid

According to the Latin poet Ovid, Arachne was a Greek peasant girl so skilled in weaving that she dared to challenge Athena, patroness of weaving, to a contest. The goddess produced a tapestry depicting her fellow OLYMPIANS in glory; Arachne, with no less skill, wove a tableau of their trysts and deceits.

Outraged by the double insult, Athena destroyed the girl's work, whereupon Arachne hanged herself. Moved to pity, the goddess turned her into a spider, as adept in spinning gossamer as the girl herself had been. Hence *Arachnida,* the class of arthropods which includes not only spiders but also scorpions, mites, and ticks.

Atlas

Atlas was one of the Titans, who made war on and were defeated by Zeus (see TITANIC). As punishment for his part in the war, Atlas was given the job of holding up the heavens forever—or in later myths, the Earth. Greek folk geography places him in northern Africa, where the Atlas mountains bear his name. In Ovid's Latin redaction that range is the Titan himself, petrified when Perseus, miffed at being denied hospitality, showed him the head of Medusa, the monster whose appearance was enough to turn any viewer into stone.

Atlas narrowly missed the opportunity to transfer his eternal burden when Hercules, seeking the golden apples of Atlas's daughters, the Hesperides, agreed to hold up the world while the Titan got the apples for him. Upon returning, Atlas refused to exchange the fruit for the sky until wily Hercules asked if, just for a moment, Atlas could resume his traditional role while he hunted up a pad for his shoulders. The gullible Titan agreed, and that was the last he saw of the hero. (See also HERCULEAN TASK.)

The term *atlas* as applied to a collection of maps dates from the sixteenth century, when such collections occasionally displayed the figure of the Titan as a frontispiece. Mapmakers John Hondt and Gerardus Mercator not only used the figure but called their most famous collection *Atlas; or a Geographic Description of the World.* A noted Renaissance geographer, Mercator was born in Flanders in 1512, introduced the still widely used *Mercator projection* in 1569, and died in 1594. The *Atlas* was published by his son a year after his death.

Augean Stables

If the latest crop of antigovernment government officials had had a passing acquaintance with world literature, they might, at the last election, have promised to "cleanse the Augean stables of federal bureaucracy." An *Augean task* is a particularly distasteful one, and an *Augean stable* is a place of great filth or corruption. The original such stable belonged to the mythological Greek king Augeas, the owner of 30,000 head of oxen whose quarters had gone unswept for thirty years. It fell to Hercules, as the fifth task set him by Eurystheus, to clean out the mess in one day (see HERCULEAN TASK), He did so by temporarily diverting two rivers from their beds so that their waters swept out the filth. Mark Twain adopts the river-diversion conceit to humorous effect in his satire "Fenimore Cooper's Literary Offenses," where he has Cooper's Indian hero Chingachgook (whom Twain calls "Chicago") turn a stream out of its course to pick up an underwater trail.

Aurora Borealis

In the northern hemisphere travelers call it *aurora borealis,* or "northern lights," for Boreas, the Greek north wind. South of the equator it is *aurora australis,* from the Latin adjective for "south." In both hemispheres the polar aurora is an undulating curtain of lights, apparently caused by the interaction between the earth's magnetic field and the solar wind. Ionized oxygen molecules produce the aurora's characteristic green hue, while nitrogen provides the contrasting reds. The combination has awed polar travelers for over 2,000 years.

In Latin *aurora* means "dawn," and in Roman mythology Aurora was the equivalent of the Greek Eos, the personification of dawn. Described by Homer as "rosy-fingered dawn," she was the mother of the four winds (including Boreas and ZEPHYR) and, in the original May-December marriage, the wife of decrepit Tithonus, a once nubile Trojan prince to whom Zeus had granted immortality—but without eternal youth to go with it. As he grew less hardy and more unhappy, Tithonus begged his wife to release him, and to terminate his anguish she turned him into a grasshopper.

As the shadowy partner to glorious dawn, Tithonus became a patron in the 1840s to certain photography enthusiasts, who gave the label *tithonicity* to the property in solar radiation that was thought responsible for chemical change, as for example in the DAGUERREOTYPE. One 1842 contributor to London's *Philosophical Magazine,* dazzled by the terms *tithonometer* (a primitive light meter), *tithonic effect,* and *diatithonescence,* distinguished neatly between the visible red light of the sun and "an invisible tithonic ray beyond the violet."

Memnon, son of Aurora and Tithonus, fought on the side of Troy against the Greeks and became the last celebrated victim of ACHILLES' prowess. According to legend, the morning dew is Aurora's tears, shed still for the loss of her son.

B

Babbitt

What a Marxist might call petty bourgeois respectability the Americans of the 1920s knew as *Babbittry*. George F. Babbitt, the protagonist of Sinclair Lewis's 1922 novel *Babbitt,* epitomized what Lewis called the Tired Business Man, the apostle of conventional tastes and "militant dullness." Babbitt, as he was introduced in the novel, "made nothing in particular, neither butter nor shoes nor poetry, but he was nimble in the calling of selling houses for more than people could afford to pay." Materialistic, smugly conformist, and mindlessly enthusiastic about his own middle-class existence, Babbitt represented all that Lewis hated about America, and *Babbittry* became a tag for these qualities.

Born in Minnesota in 1885, Lewis graduated from Yale in 1908, worked as a journalist for several years, and became an instant phenomenon in 1920 with his sixth novel, *Main Street.* The first of his many novels to score the complacent provincialism of American life, it was received, in the words of Lewis's biographer Mark Schorer, as "the most sensational event in twentieth-century publishing history." Lewis himself remarked years later, "Some hundreds of thousands read the book with the same masochistic pleasure that one has in sucking an aching tooth." Next came *Babbitt,* and then a triad of realistic masterpieces in which Lewis turned his critical gaze to the medical establishment (*Arrowsmith,* 1925), popular religion (*Elmer Gantry,* 1927), and the contrast between American and European values (*Dodsworth,* 1929).

Lewis turned down the PULITZER PRIZE for *Arrowsmith* in 1926, explaining that he did not wish to contribute to a system that encouraged writers to become "safe, polite, obedient, and sterile." Four years later, however, he accepted the NOBEL PRIZE for literature—the first American to be so honored. Throughout the 1930s he was married to the celebrated columnist Dorothy Thompson. His writings of that period were less fervent, and less fervently received, than his earlier books, although he did produce a chilling prophecy of American fascism in the 1935 *It Can't Happen Here*. In his later years he lived mostly in New England, and he died in 1951 on a trip to Rome.

Babbitt, incidentally, was a distinguished American name before Lewis's novel besmirched it. Elijah Babbitt (1795–1887) was a Republican congressman from Pennsylvania. Isaac Babbitt (1799–1862) made the first Britannia ware and the first brass cannon in the United States, and also invented the antifriction alloy known as *babbitt metal*. Benjamin Talbot Babbitt (1808–89), another inventor, patented over a hundred mechanical devices, including the country's first pump fire engine, and was also the first entrepreneur to use free samples in advertising. None of them was guilty of Babbittry.

Barbie Doll

The Barbie doll was introduced by the Mattel Toy Company in 1959, and it may not be coincidental that the book which sparked modern feminism, Betty Friedan's *Feminine Mystique,* appeared only four years later. In the comfortable old baby doll era, the message of doll ownership was maternal: when you grow up, you'll get to change diapers. Since 1959, girls have been hearing a more adult message: you'll also get to doll up for male gawkers—here's a full-figured mannequin to practice on.

The little plastic clothes horse that turned Mattel into the biggest toy firm in the world was the brainchild of company founders Ruth and Elliot Handler, who noticed deep in the Eisenhower years that their daughter Barbie preferred teenage cutout dolls to the then rampant burpers and cooers. Barbie Handler thus inspired the original fashion doll; two years later, in 1961, her brother became the prototype of Ken. In the ensuing quarter century, this dapper duo has spawned dozens of diversifications (Barbie's sister Skipper, Fashion Photo Barbie, Great Shape Ken), thousands of collectors, and an explosion in *couture de poupée*. Not to mention 200 million dolls in the Barbie "family." Laid end to end, the company boasts, they could orbit the earth four times. Which brings to mind Dorothy Parker's quip: "If all the starlets in Hollywood were laid end to end . . . I wouldn't be a bit surprised."

Bartlett's Quotations

In spite of twentieth-century competition, John Bartlett's *Familiar Quotations,* first published in 1855, remains the bibliophile's crib of choice when tracking down obscure attributions. Born in Plymouth, Massachusetts, Bartlett (1820–1905) began working at the Harvard University bookstore in Cambridge as a teenager, eventually becoming both the store's owner and a walking bookstore himself. A notebook in which he kept track of customers' queries about literature grew into the first edition of his miscellany, and the Cantabrigian counsel "Ask John Bartlett" took on national relevance. From 1863 on Bartlett worked for the Boston publishing firm Little, Brown, which brought out numerous editions of the *Quotations* both before and after his death. His other writings include books on fishing and chess and a concordance to Shakespeare which was his generation's standard.

Beau Brummel

Beau Brummel, the epithet for a fastidious dresser, was originally the nickname of the London-born dandy George Bryan Brummel (1778–1840), who at the turn of the nineteenth century dramatically altered English fashion. Brummel's reputation for conversational and sartorial elegance was established at Eton, where, although a commoner himself, he mingled with the aristocracy, including the Prince of Wales, the heir to the English throne.

Commissioned in the Prince's regiment at sixteen, Brummel rose rapidly to a captaincy, and in 1798, having inherited a fortune, he left the army to pursue more sophisticated pleasures in London. For the next two decades, in that peculiarly etiolated branch of society that made leisure the excuse for its existence, Brummel was an uncrowned king.

Although he was known for his cutting repartee as well as for the cut of his coats, his rhetorical skills do not shine through in surviving anecdotes: it is difficult to see why even the British aristocracy would consider his famous swipe "Do you call that thing a coat?" an example of wit. His renown as an arbiter of fashion is better founded, if somewhat distorted in retrospect by the contemporary connotations of "dandy." Finicky Brummel may have been, but he was certainly no fop. In fact, he initiated a movement away from the multihued frippery of the eighteenth century and toward the lean lines and subdued colors of the nineteenth. Inventor of the starched neckcloth, he is also credited (wrongly) with the abolition of the powdered wig and (rightly) with the introduction of long PANTS.

Brummel exercised a SVENGALI-like hold on the Prince of Wales until about 1812, when the Prince's new status as regent, coupled with some ill-chosen words by the Beau, ended the association and undercut Brummel's primacy in society. Four years later, deeply in debt to gamblers, he moved to France, where he held a brief consular sinecure, accumulated more debts, spent a summer in prison, and, toward the end of his life, became gradually more slovenly and incompetent. In his fifties he took to holding phantom receptions for the illustrious companions of his youth, and he died in an asylum for the insane.

Berserk

Berserk, which in Old Norse means "bear shirt," was an ancient Scandinavian hero so fiercely reckless of danger that he battled not in armor but in bearskins. Warriors who adopted this practice were known as *berserks* or *berserkers,* and at a time when personal combat was at a particularly ferocious pitch, they were the wildest of the wild. H. R. Ellis Davidson, in her *Gods and Myths of Northern Europe,* says they were inspired by Odin and quotes a saga describing their behavior: they were "frantic as dogs or wolves; they bit their shields and were as strong as bears or boars; they slew men, but neither fire nor iron could hurt them." Hence *berserk,* meaning "raging" or "crazed."

Bessemer Process

Although ironworking was an established craft among the Hittites thirty-five centuries ago, steel production was a fitful phenomenon until the mid-nineteenth century. Steel *is* iron, of course—a strong, resilient, and relatively "pure" iron from which most of the natural carbon has been removed. For centuries the decarbonizing, or refining, process involved heating iron with charcoal in small and inefficient crucibles; the resulting steel production was minuscule.

What changed that was the Bessemer conversion process. English metalworker Henry Bessemer (1813–98) spent the first forty years of his life inventing manufacturing devices, including a type compositor, a ventilator, and a process for pulverizing metals. During the Crimean War, he studied ways to improve the quality of cannon iron. He presented his results to the British scientific community in 1856 and, a year later, patented the process that bears his name.

The Bessemer process should really be called the Kelly-Bessemer process, for the American John Kelly (1811–88) had discovered and patented it in 1851. Its operating principle is that air blown through molten iron will oxidize the metal's impurities (including carbon), thus producing molten steel. Kelly's pneumatic purification method lacked a practical container in which to heat, and from which to pour, the hot metal. Bessemer's tilting "converter," part of his 1857 patent, was that essential component, and after some bitter legal wrangling, the two men merged their companies in the 1860s. For his part in the development, Bessemer was knighted in 1879.

The Bessemer conversion process, first used in a Michigan refinery in 1864, was a boon to the railroad industry, in the making of steel rails, and to manufacturing in general. By the turn of the century, however, it was already being supplanted by the Siemens-Martin open hearth process, which produced higher-grade steel from poorer scrap iron. It is virtually defunct today.

Big Ben

The tower clock of London's Houses of Parliament is commonly called Big Ben, but it is actually the clock's largest bell, a thirteen-ton giant cast in the mid-1850s, to which the name originally referred. Cecil Hunt, in his *Word Origins,* says it was to have been called "St. Stephen" until a random press usage identified it with the government's chief commissioner of works, Sir Benjamin Hall, and the sobriquet "Big Ben" stuck.

A career politician from Wales, Hall (1802–67) served in the House of Commons from 1832 to 1859, then, having been made Lord Llanover, in the House of Lords until 1863. A champion of the Welsh liturgy, he was long associated with ecclesiastical reform and, during his tenure as works commissioner (1855–58), with the improvement of London's parks. A bill he introduced in Parliament in 1855 led to the establishment of the first metropolitan board of works—an initiative which makes his eponymous connection with London's best-known landmark quite fitting.

Bloomers

Amelia Jenks Bloomer (1818–94) was an American feminist and reformer who started one of the first women's magazines, *The Lily*, in 1849. As its editor she championed temperance and a range of feminist causes, including education for girls, reform of the marriage laws, and female suffrage. Elizabeth Cady Stanton contributed work to the magazine, and by 1853 Bloomer was reaching 4,000 subscribers. The success of *The Lily,* however, was attributable in considerable part to the support given in its pages to a relatively trivial, and certainly distracting, cause: that of women's dress reform. In the 1850s, as in the 1960s, feminist fashion tended not so much to heighten as to obscure an understanding of more critical issues.

The fashion in question was the Bloomer Costume or, more simply, *bloomers,* consisting of a short skirt over baggy Turkish-style PANTALOONS. The actress Fanny Kemble wore such a costume in 1849, and the reformer Elizabeth Smith Miller had introduced it to Stanton in 1851. Bloomer picked it up around this time; promoted it in her magazine as the fitting dress for a modern, unconstrained woman; wore it on her own speaking engagements; and was deluged by letters from readers requesting patterns. To those who saw all feminist designs as scandalous, bloomers became the living proof that what "these women" really wanted was to dress up and play at being men. It was as if the demands of black radicals in the 1960s could be reduced to the Afro and dashiki.

The bloomer fad passed around 1853, and Bloomer moved with her husband to the Midwest. She sold *The Lily,* settled in Council Bluffs, Iowa, and continued to write and lecture, in semi-exile, until her death.

Blurb

Blurb, the book industry's term for the frequently puffed-up encomia that grace the jackets of newly published volumes, was coined by the American humorist and illustrator Gelett Burgess (1866–1951). According to Charles Earle Funke's *Thereby Hangs a Tale,* the word dates from 1907, when at a booksellers' dinner the publisher distributed copies of Burgess's *Are You a Bromide?* adorned with a special jacket designed by the author. Following the custom of the day for new novels, the jacket pictured a young woman—in this case, a "sickly sweet young woman . . . lifted from a Lydia Pinkham or tooth-powder advertisement." To her picture the author had added his own embellishments and a text applauding her beauty. The model's name, Burgess wrote, was Miss Belinda Blurb.

Burgess wrote over thirty-five books but was notorious in his day for a single whimsical quatrain:

I never saw a purple cow.
I never hope to see one.
But I can tell you anyhow,
I'd rather see than be one.

That innocent toss-off, published in the inaugural issue of Burgess's little magazine *The Lark,* came to haunt the writer, who became so weary of hearing it quoted that he later added this rejoinder:

Ah, yes, I wrote the "Purple Cow."
I'm sorry, now, I wrote it.
But I can tell you anyhow,
I'll kill you if you quote it!

It was no use. Throughout his life Burgess was linked to those telling four lines, and as late as 1961 a biographer saw fit to identify his subject as "the man who wrote the 'Purple Cow.' "

This is more the pity because Burgess's other contributions to popular culture were considerable. Born in Boston, he attended M.I.T. and in the late 1880s moved to San Francisco, where he taught briefly at Berkeley before becoming an editor on the society paper *The Wave*. For decades, living first in San Francisco and, after 1897, in New York, he was a fixture on the literary scene, contributing to magazines as varied as the fashionable *Smart Set,* the juvenile *St. Nicholas,* and the left-wing *Masses*. His briskly satirical style is suggested by the titles of some of his books: in addition to *Are You a Bromide?* they include *Why Men Hate Women* (1927) and *Look Eleven Years Younger* (1937).

Fond of inventing his own words, Burgess also gave the American language *goop* (for an ill-mannered boor), *spuzz* (for stamina or spice) and *varm* (for the essence of sex). Today, only *blurb* survives.

Bobby

The distinguished career of Sir Robert Peel (1788–1850) is memorialized in two rather misleading idioms: the popular tag *bobby* for a London policeman and the less affectionate underworld *peeler,* meaning any officer of the law.

One of the most imaginative and controversial figures in British politics, Peel began his parliamentary career as a hard-line Tory and ended it by repealing the Corn Laws, which, by maintaining high tariffs for imported grain, had long consolidated the wealth of Tory landowners. Son of a successful mill owner, Peel entered Parliament in 1809, and as Irish secretary from 1812 to 1818 so antagonized the Catholic population that he was referred to as Orange Peel. In 1829, however, he began to pursue a more conciliatory policy, even supporting a Catholic suffrage act, which effectively isolated him from the Tories and led him, in 1834, to found the reform-minded Conservative Party. In November of that year Peel became England's first Conservative prime minister.

Peel twice more headed the government in the 1840s, advocating free trade, establishing a national banking system, and fighting an unpopular battle for Irish relief after the 1845 famine. When he advocated repeal of the Corn Laws, his political ship was sunk. He left the government in 1846 and was killed four years later in a riding accident.

Peel had established the first successful constabularies in Ireland (during his secretaryship there) and London (as home secretary in 1828): hence, respectively, peeler and bobby. It is a sad commentary on selective memory that someone who had worked so hard for reform should be popularly remembered by two words that evoke only his pre-Conservative, "law and order" career.

Bowdlerize

The verb *to bowdlerize,* meaning "to expurgate," owes its existence to the popularity of one much vilified book, an excessively weeded version of the Bard's plays known as *The Family Shakespeare.* On the title page of the 1818 edition, the editor, retired physician Thomas Bowdler (1754–1825), gave the reader fair warning: "Nothing is added to the text; but those expressions are omitted which cannot with propriety be read aloud in a family." Which meant that most references to sex, and all but the most reverent allusions to God, had been expunged. It was Shakespeare without the spice, and in the Victorian age this was exactly what the reading classes wanted: by the end of the century, fifty expurgated Shakespeares were competing with the good doctor's work.

Bowdler's family shared his prudish zeal, and Noel Perrin, in his book *Dr. Bowdler's Legacy,* makes a good case for the view that Thomas should share the fame, or the infamy, of having torn Shakespeare to shreds with other members of the clan. His father, Squire Thomas Bowdler, had died in 1785, but his evening readings of Shakespeare to his children, the younger Thomas once acknowledged, had inspired his own brave excisions. Also deserving of credit might be Thomas's siblings, especially his sister Harriet.

Harriet, Perrin claims, was most likely the phantom editor of the original *Family Shakespeare,* an 1807 edition obscurely printed at Bath. In zealousness brother and sister were well matched. His hand was usually heavier than hers, but his 1818 edition did include a purified *Romeo and Juliet;* her 1807 edition had dropped that naughty play altogether.

After the success of *The Family Shakespeare,* Thomas Bowdler turned his hand to Gibbon. He worked at trimming the English historian's *Decline and Fall of the Roman Empire* until his death. *The Family Gibbon* was published posthumously a year later; it never sold out its first edition.

Bowie Knife

Credit for the invention of the *Bowie knife,* or "Arkansas toothpick," generally goes to James Bowie (1796–1836), who is supposed to have come up with the design, featuring a heavy guard between the hilt and the blade, after he had cut himself in a fight. Some authorities, however, give the nod to James's brother Rezin (1793–1841), following a Louisiana legend that has him cutting *his* hand in trying to slaughter a cow. Whichever story is correct, it was James who made the weapon famous when, in September

1827 near Natchez, he used it to kill a pistol-wielding rival in a duel.

James's capture of popular credit for the knife may be attributed partly to the Natchez fight and partly to the fact that, unlike his older brother, he later became a martyr at the Alamo: the image of the gallant Texas hero, slashing at Mexicans from his cot, is so resonant in our popular culture that it seems niggling to call attention to absent Rezin.

Even before that final tableau, James's life had provided plenty of material for romance-mongers. As a teenager growing up in Louisiana, he gained a reputation for fearlessness by roping and riding not just wild horses, but alligators as well. In the 1820s he sold fraudulent Arkansas land grants and, although the Bowie family has always denied it, seems to have formed a slave-smuggling ring with Rezin, John Bowie (another brother), and the pirate Jean Lafitte. In Texas after 1828, he became a Mexican citizen, married the daughter of the province's vice-governor, searched for a fabled lost mine, and, by duping Mexicans into serving as middlemen, acquired huge tracts of Texas land. A colorful if not entirely ethical adventurer, he joined the Texas revolutionary forces in 1832 and four years later, as co-commander of the Alamo with William B. Travis, met his fate at the hands of Santa Anna's soldiers. Within a few years after his death, the Bowie knife was being mass marketed for the Texas trade by the famous Sheffield steelworks in England.

Boycott

The boycott, a refusal to transact business with personal or political antagonists, has figured in public affairs for centuries. The Boston Tea Party, for example, was a forcible and extreme boycott against suppliers of English tea. The term itself, however, is more recent. It arose in Ireland in the 1880s, at a time when crop failures and the insensitivity of absentee landlords were aggravating the already hard lot of tenant farmers, driving them toward eviction.

Many of those evicted had had insult added to injury when new tenants took over their farms, and to discourage such agrarian scabbing the Irish nationalist leader Charles Parnell in September 1880 urged a tenant group to isolate the newcomers completely, as if each were "a leper of old." Starting with this modest proposal, farmers soon began to ostracize all their enemies, including most notably a land agent called Charles Boycott, who had refused to liberalize his tenants' onerous rent payment schedules. In retaliation they refused to gather his crops, intimidated his servants, intercepted his mail, tore down his fences, hung him in effigy, and made threats upon his life. The term *boycott* was quickly adopted not only in the British Isles but throughout Europe to describe such intimidating tactics. Modern tongues retain the usage, as in German *Boykott,* Spanish *boicot,* and French *boycottage.*

Ironically, although Boycott's name survives as a synonym for active discrimination against opponents, he was himself the passive object of the practice. Far from implementing the original boycott, he was actually its victim.

Braille

The Braille system of writing is so widely known to the general public that it is easy to forget that, for thousands of years after the invention of writing, the blind could not read at all. Until the nineteenth century, the only touch-reading technology in existence was a method using enlarged and raised lettering that had been developed at France's Institut National des Jeunes Aveugles, and it was severely hampered by its reliance on oversized texts. The person who changed that, and opened the world of writing to the blind, was a remarkable Frenchman named Louis Braille.

Blinded in an accident at the age of three, Braille (1809–52) was educated with sighted children and managed to keep up with the class by employing an extremely retentive memory. At ten he was sent to the Paris-based institute for the blind, where he witnessed a demonstration by army officer Charles Barbier of a battlefield night communication system composed of embossed dots and dashes. Braille simplified Barbier's rather cumbersome model, transforming it into the now familiar *Braille cell,* in which raised dots, located in one or more of six positions, are arranged in patterns indicating the letters of the alphabet and numerals. In spite of resistance from sighted teachers, Braille introduced his method at the school in 1824, when he was only fifteen, and published it five years later.

As a teacher at the school from 1826, Braille also introduced the stylus and punch-card apparatus for blind writing, and for the remainder of his life he continued to make improvements to his system, among them notational variations for music (he was an organist and cellist), science, and mathematics. Similar systems challenged his primacy in the 1830s and after, but today's standardized Braille is a direct descendant of the teenaged founder's six-position design.

Bunsen Burner

Robert Wilhelm Bunsen (1811–99) was a prodigious inventor and for nearly half a century professor of chemistry at Heidelberg University. Known especially for pioneering work in spectrum analysis, he also did research on gases, and in 1857 published a standard text on the measurement of gas volumes. Among his many practical contributions were the grease-spot photometer, ice and vapor calorimeters, and the carbon-zinc electric cell. His most famous device, however, was the gas burner that carries his name. Still the standard laboratory burner, it gives off a hot but nonluminous flame when a mixture of gas and air is ignited in a vertical tube. Bunsen is generally given sole credit for the design, although he actually derived it from models that had been proposed by, among others, Michael Faraday.

Buridan's Ass

Jean Buridan (1300–58) was a scholastic philosopher whose commentaries on Aristotle commanded wide attention in the Middle Ages, even beyond the borders of his native France. Like all medieval thinkers, Buridan was captivated by the notion of free will; on this subject he argued that reason constrains us to choose whatever appears as the greatest good, but that our will is free to delay this necessary choice pending a full inquiry into options. The potential hazards of this delaying function are illustrated in the allegory of Buridan's ass.

Suppose an ass is placed in a field between two identical piles of hay, and suppose the animal, in deciding between them, uses not instinct but reason. According to Buridan's logic, the creature will starve to death, unable to make either choice because neither pile is better than the other. From this celebrated anecdote, a *Buridan's ass* came to mean anyone undone by indecision. Ironically, nowhere in Buridan's writings does this starved-ass story appear. He does have a dog face the dilemma, but the dog doesn't end up starving; instead it chooses a pile of food at random. Just what any jackass would have done.

A Bouquet of Botanists

Horticulturists are inordinately fond of immortalizing themselves in the names of the plants they develop or discover. Usually they appropriate the species or variety label, so that botanical catalogues are full of classifications like *Rosa willmottiae, Dianthus allwoodii,* and *Tulipa kaufmanniana*. Occasionally some lucky soul gets an entire genus named for him; yet, ironically, in these cases the Latinized surname soon becomes so common that its origin is forgotten. Some common examples, with the people whose names they bear:

begonia — Michel Begon, a seventeenth-century French botanist and onetime governor of Santo Domingo

camellia — George Joseph Kamel, who brought the first specimens to Europe from the East in the seventeenth century

dahlia — A Swedish doctor named Andreas Dahl, who was a botanist and a student of the great Linneaus

forsythia — William Forsyth, who brought the plant from China at the beginning of the nineteenth century

fuchsia — The sixteenth-century German botanist Leonhart Fuchs, who in addition to his horticultural work was professor of medicine at Tübingen University gardenia Dr. Alexander Garden, a Scottish immigrant who became a specialist in the botany of the Blue Ridge Mountains

gentian Gentius (according to Pliny), king of the ancient Adriatic country of Illyria

magnolia Pierre Magnol, seventeenth-century professor of botany at the university in Montpelier, France

poinsettia Martin Van Buren's secretary of war, Joel Roberts Poinsett, also a congressman and diplomat, who as minister to Mexico introduced the plant to the United States

wistaria Caspar Wistar, professor of anatomy in the early nineteenth century at the College of Pennsylvania

zinnia Dr. J. G. Zinn, eighteenth-century professor of medicine at the German university of Göttingen

Note also a trio of flowers named for mythological characters, all of whom shared an unfortunate aptitude for incurring divine wrath:

hyacinth A Greek youth beloved of Apollo and ZEPHYR, god of the west wind. Scorned in favor of Apollo, Zephyr killed the lad, and from his spilled blood the flower grew.

iris A young girl with the bad taste to catch lusty Zeus's eye. Jealous Hera, Zeus's much abused wife, turned her into a rainbow, and it was from the "rainbow goddess" that the flower took its name.

narcissus Another pretty face done wrong, Narcissus rejected the advances of ECHO and was punished for it by NEMESIS, who made him fall in love with his own reflection in a fountain. Unable to consummate the union, he wasted away into the flower. Hence the clinical term for self-absorption, *narcissism*.

C

Casanova

A *Casanova* in modern usage is an unprincipled and profligate ladies' man, and although the original Casanova did fit that description, he was a jack of more than one trade whose reputation was distorted, ironically, by his own scurrilous memoirs.

Born into a theatrical family in Venice, Giovanni Giacomo Casanova (1725–98) began his scandalous career in a seminary, from which he was expelled in his teens. As a young man he played violin in a Venetian theater, dabbled in freemasonry, served a Roman cardinal, and broke hearts and bank accounts from Paris to Prague. Imprisoned by Venetian authorities for witchcraft in 1755, he escaped and returned to Paris, where he made a quick reputation as a squanderer of his own and other people's money: in 1757 he introduced the lottery to France. Subsequent travels brought him into contact with many Enlightenment notables, including Voltaire, the magician Cagliostro, Catherine the Great of Russia, and Prussia's Frederick the Great, who was impressed enough to offer him employment. In the 1770s he served his old NEMESIS, the Venetian state, as a spy, and for his last thirteen years was librarian, in a quiet chateau, to a Bohemian nobleman.

Casanova's Bohemian seclusion produced the memoirs for which he is remembered, and which provide an entertaining panorama not only of his own amorous escapades but of all eighteenth-century society. His literary interests, however, as befitted the ingenious *dilettanti* of the era, displayed an extremely wide scope. His other writings include opera libretti, political satires, a translation of the *Iliad,* poetry, and a visionary picaresque novel called *Icosameron* which, anticipating Jules Verne, tells of adventures at the center of the earth.

Celsius Scale

The Celsius temperature scale is named for Anders Celsius (1701–44), a Swedish astronomer whose 1742 paper on the "two constant degrees" of a thermometer popularized the 100-degree scale throughout Europe. He assigned to his two "constants," the boiling and freezing points of water, the values of 0 and 100, respectively; later reversed, these became the "end points" of the decimal-type temperature scale still used universally by scientists. Known first as the "Swedish thermometer," the scale was called *centigrade* until 1948, when a world conference on weights and measures changed the name officially to *Celsius*.

The son of an astronomy professor, Celsius taught mathematics for several years until, in 1730, he was made professor of astronomy at the University of Uppsala. He helped to build Sweden's first modern observatory there, published observations of the AURORA BOREALIS, and in 1736–37 performed meridian measurements in Lapland, confirming Isaac Newton's hypothesis that the earth was slightly flattened at the poles.

Cereal

Ceres, the ancient Roman goddess of agriculture, was patroness particularly of grain, or cereal, plants: the Latin adjective *cerealis* means "relating to Ceres." She was equivalent to the Greek goddess Demeter, the Hellenic version of that oldest and most widely revered of all deities, the Earth Mother. Worshipped in the Greeks' most sacred religious festival, the spring and fall mysteries at Eleusis, Demeter was protectress of all vegetation, and as such wielded great power. When her brother Hades, god of the underworld, abducted her daughter, Persephone, she withered every plant on the earth until he agreed to give her up. In a compromise similar to, but much older than, that of the ADONIS myth, Persephone was allowed to spend half the year underground and half on the earth with her mother. Thus the Greeks explained the cycle of the seasons.

Chauvinism

If patriotism, as Dr. Johnson claimed, is the last refuge of the scoundrel, Nicolas Chauvin was a scoundrel in spades. A soldier in Napoleon's army, he was wounded repeatedly during the Corsican's push for power and upon his retirement earned a reputation in his village of Rochefort for unbridled devotion to the defeated emperor. First admired and then ridiculed for his zeal, Chauvin became the paragon of blind allegiance to a leader, a cause, a mother soil.

Chauvinism might have remained a local, transient expression but for two theatrical brothers, Charles and Jean Cogniard, whose 1831 comedy *La cocarde tricolore* (The Tricolored Cockade) featured the veteran Chauvin, smitten to comic effect with what the staid Larousse later called "idolatrie napoléonienne." The popularity of this play was what made *chauvinism* a popular synonym for knee-jerk patriotism. The feminist usage of the term, to deride attitudes of male supremacy, arose in the 1970s.

Chauvinism is often used interchangeably (and laxly) with "jingoism," a noneponymous term which derives from the expression "By jingo," popularized by an 1878 song extolling the virtues of British imperialism. Used first to describe London's hard-line stance against the Russian bear in Turkey, "jingoism" soon came to mean any bellicose, posturing attitude in international affairs. It was, and remains, chauvinism with a snarl.

Crapper

The case of Thomas Crapper, the scatophile's favorite son, illustrates a kind of eponymy in reverse. A London-born engineer,

Crapper was the inventor of something called the valveless water-waste preventer, which utilized a floating ball mechanism in a precursor of the modern flush toilet. The vulgarism *crapper,* however, does not come from Thomas's family name. It was in use as a synonym for privy, that is, a place to defecate, probably as early as the eighteenth century—so says slang expert Eric Partridge. Crapper lived a hundred years later, at the height of the Victorian era; he demonstrated his marvel, which helped to revolutionize indoor plumbing, at an 1884 British health exhibition. It was a bizarre eponymological accident that linked his name to the medieval *crappe,* which was related to crop and referred to various kinds of refuse, especially chaff. Had the genealogical cards been dealt differently, we might now know the toilet as a "chaffer."

Craps

To throw *craps* in the game of that name is to go bust with a two, three, or twelve. Robert Hendrickson, in a coy tale that is too good not to repeat, suggests the term may derive from "Johnny Crapaud," the nickname of a French gambler, Bernard Marigny, who was supposed to have introduced dice into New Orleans around 1800. *Crapaud,* he says, was also a common epithet for any Frenchman: the word means "toad," and may have referred to "the belief that three *crapauds* or toads were the ancient arms of France." Or, one might further suppose, to the Frenchman's fondness for frogs.

This tale has color to recommend it, but not much else. According to the *Oxford English Dictionary, craps* is a variant of *crabs,* which was used in English as early as 1768 to indicate the lowest throw at dice: a pair of ones. (Why *crabs* not even the *OED* knows; clearly "snake eyes" is visually more appropriate.) The association of "Johnny Toad" with the term almost certainly came after the fact.

Jim Crow Laws

The segregated South—that phantasmagorical wasteland of "colored" lunch counters, schoolrooms, and drinking fountains—was not a creation of slavery, as is often supposed, but of the 1890s. Until then the two races in the South, both before and after the Civil War, were actually far less separated than they ever had been in the North. What changed this at the turn of the century was an agreement among disappointed populists, southern conservatives, and conciliatory northerners to blame the Negro menace for America's economic ills. The result was a vast network of "Jim Crow" laws that were not nullified until the Civil Rights Act of 1964.

Although Jim Crow legislation arose only in the 1890s, however, the use of the term *Jim Crow* to refer to blacks goes back much further. "Jim Crow" was the stage persona of Thomas Dartmouth Rice, a traveling song-and-dance man who has been called "the father of American minstrelsy." Rice introduced his Jim Crow character at a Louisville theater in 1828 and scored an instant hit. For the next twenty years, his song "Jump Jim Crow" and the accompanying hopping dance were staples on the blackface circuit, and "Daddy" Rice was a theatrical phenomenon on both sides of the Atlantic. Before the craze died down, *Jim Crow* had come to refer not just to Rice's dancing darky caricature but to blacks in general.

Rice's success in the Jim Crow role fostered a rash of imitators and was indirectly responsible for the "Ethiopian delineators" and full-fledged minstrel shows of the mid-nineteenth century. Rice himself performed other blackface roles (including that of UNCLE TOM) throughout the 1850s, squandered most of his fortune, and died just before the Civil War.

Cyrillic Alphabet

The Cyrillic alphabet used for modern Russian, Bulgarian, Ukranian, and Serbian is traditionally credited to the Greek missionary saint Cyril (ca. 827–69). In fact the script he invented was probably the related but cursive Glagolitic; modern scholars say that the uncial-form Cyrillic replaced it only after his death. But whatever the linguistic particulars, it is clear that Cyril (known as Constantine in his lifetime) did bring the eastern Slavs their first alphabet, thus creating a foundation for their literature.

Born in Thessalonika, Constantine moved to Constantinople, capital of the Byzantine empire, at fourteen, to study philosophy. He became the protégé of the imperial minister Theoctistos, was ordained a priest, earned a reputation as a theological debater, and was appointed librarian to Hagia Sophia. After Theoctistos's assassination in 855, Constantine left the city to join his younger brother, Methodius, in a monastery in Asia Minor. There they might have remained in seclusion had not their skill in oratory suggested them as missionaries.

In 860, Constantine and Methodius were sent on the first of two evangelistic journeys, to the country of the Khazars near the Caspian Sea. Little is known of that journey except that they returned through the Crimea, where they secured what they believed to be relics of Pope Clement I. The second journey, to what is now Czechoslovakia, is better recorded. To proclaim his ecclesiastical and political autonomy from his Frankish neighbors to the west, Prince Ratislav of Moravia in 862 petitioned the Byzantine emperor to send him priests who could instruct his people in the Christian liturgy, but in their own tongue. The task fell to Constantine and Methodius, who had learned the language in their youth.

In preparation for the mission, the brothers composed a Slavic alphabet into which they translated the Gospels. In Moravia in 863, using this foundation, they created a full Slavic liturgy and attracted a cadre of disciples. In spite of resistance from the German clergy, who saw them as interlopers, the new liturgy was approved by the pope in 867 and, in a nod to the vulgate which anticipated Vatican II by eleven centuries, was celebrated throughout Rome. His magnum opus accomplished, Constantine took a monk's habit, adopted the name Cyril, and died two years later. Methodius continued apostolic work among the Slavs until his own death in 885.

Clothing: A (Mostly English) Wardrobe

argyle This diamond-patterned plaid, often seen in sweaters and socks, adapts the traditional green and white tartan of the Campbell clan, which hails from the Scottish county of Argyllshire.

cardigan The collarless V-necked cardigan sweater was named for the seventh earl of Cardigan, who wore a similar garment during the Crimean War, when he commanded the famous Light Brigade.

Eisenhower jacket A waist-length, close-fitting jacket that was standard issue during World War II, it became associated with Ike because he was European theater commander.

jersey This athlete's special was named for the English Channel island of Jersey, where such knit garments were traditionally made. The island's name is the anglicized form of (Julius) Caesar, who conquered Britain in the first century B.C.

leotard	The dancer's standard bodysuit was named for Jules Léotard (1838–70), a French acrobat who introduced the revolutionary attire in an 1859 Paris circus act.
mackintosh	This slang term for a raincoat comes from Charles Macintosh (1766–1843), the Scottish chemist and Royal Society fellow who in 1823 patented the first practical waterproof cloth.
Nehru jacket	Popularized briefly in the 1960s by London's Carnaby Street, the short-necked traditional Indian jacket was named for Jawaharlal Nehru, prime minister of India from 1947 until his death in 1964.
raglan sleeves	Sleeves seamed on a bias to the neck are called raglan after the first baron of Raglan (1788–1855), who was Wellington's aide-de-camp at Waterloo and succeeded him as British army commander.
Wellingtons	Over-the-calf riding boots, these are named for the duke of Wellington (1769–1852), hero of Waterloo. A legend says Queen Victoria mocked the name on the grounds of improbability: there couldn't possibly, she said, be *two* Wellingtons.
Windsor knot	This bulky knot for men's ties was associated with, and thus named after, the British duke of Windsor (Edward VIII), who abdicated his throne in 1936 to make Wallace Simpson his duchess.

D

Daguerreotype

The early photographic plates named for Louis J. M. Daguerre (1787–1851) were the outcome of scientific inquiry that reached back into antiquity. It had been known since Euclid's time that light passing through a pinhole would cast a reverse image of objects on a screen. The knowledge had permitted early observation of solar eclipses, and late Renaissance artists had used it in constructing the sketching aid known as the *camera obscura*. By the late nineteenth century the idea of "fixing" the "camera's" image permanently had become the *idée fixe* of many amateur scientists.

The chief contenders for the honor of being called the father of "permanent" photography were Daguerre, the Englishman Henry Fox Talbot, and Daguerre's countrymen Hippolye Bayard and Nicéphore Niepce. The success of Daguerre's process is testimony as much to good connections as to his obvious industry. Trained as a painter and stage designer, he had worked since the early 1820s as a showman, exhibiting revolving panoramic views in his Diorama theater—a project that, fortuitously, brought him to the attention of the French government. It was government sponsorship of his metal-plate process that, in 1839, led to international acclaim. Of the other contenders, Daguerre's former partner Niepce had died in 1833; Bayard was persuaded by the French Academy of Sciences to withhold his own paper-print method to avoid confusing the public; and Talbot was merely an Englishman.

With the coffers of Paris behind him, Daguerre publicized his discovery ably, and daguerreotypes rapidly became so popular that French painter Paul Delaroche was moved to exclaim, "From now on, painting is dead." In spite of its high fidelity, however, the daguerreotype had the significant drawback of being nonreplicable, and it was gradually replaced by Talbot's calotype process, which could produce multiple prints from a single negative. Talbot in turn was displaced by his countryman Frederick Scott Archer, whose 1851 wet-plate process also produced multiple images but was sharper in detail than the calotype.

Sword of Damocles

When opponents of the arms race refer to the "nuclear umbrella" as a *sword of Damocles* in disguise, they are using a metaphor of great antiquity: the sword of Damocles has been an image of impending doom for about 2,400 years.

Damocles was a courtier in ancient Sicily. At least the kinder writers call him that; his harsher judges say "sycophant" or "flatterer." The person it was his job to flatter was Dionysius the Elder, an able general and politician who in the fifth century B.C. was sole ruler—the ancient term is "tyrant"—of the city-state of Syracuse. Being tyrant was not as good as it looked. One day, when Damocles was expounding on the felicities of the ruler's life, Dionysius asked him if he would like to sample that life himself. Of course, the courtier replied—whereupon Dionysius ordered that a vast banquet be prepared, that Damocles be laid on a bed of solid gold, that he be perfumed and garlanded and massaged, and that his every whim be met by a bevy of the tyrant's servants. There was only one catch. Directly above Damocles's head, Dionysius suspended a huge sword, secured to the royal ceiling by only a single hair. The courtier soon abandoned the feast.

The Damocles story is often told as a comment on the anxieties of command: "Uneasy lies the head that wears a crown," Shakespeare puts it in *Henry IV*. Obviously this was Dionysius's point. But the tale has wider implications. Cicero, in his *Tusculan Disputations,* uses it to illustrate the principle that no one can be happy if he lives under constant apprehension; the same principle is being invoked today by opponents of the nuclear option.

Decibel

Defined in 1937 by an International Acoustic Congress in Paris, the *decibel* is our commonest measure of sound intensity. There are technical, nonsubjective definitions of the term, but the easiest way to understand its meaning is to note that a sound of zero decibels is barely audible to the normal human ear, and one of 130 or 140 decibels is painful. Conversation takes place at about 60 decibels, while a medium-sized missile launch may thunder in at about 200.

The term is named for Alexander Graham Bell, the father of the modern telephone and the *éminence grise* behind the concept "Ma Bell." Born in Scotland in 1847, Bell moved in 1870 to America, where—as he had in his native country—he made his living as a teacher of the deaf (both his mother and his wife were deaf). It was while he was a professor of vocal physiology at Boston University that he began the electrical experiments that would make him famous. His widely heralded—and widely disputed—patent for an "Improvement in Telegraphy" was granted in the spring of 1876; on March 10 of that year, Bell spilled acid on himself in his laboratory, uttered the line "Mr. Watson, come here, I want you," and thus made possible the biggest single business in the world.

Much of Bell's energies in the 1880s and 1890s went into defending his patent and consolidating the power of the company that would eventually become AT&T. But he left time for his scientific interests. In 1880 he became a founder of the influential magazine *Science,* and from 1898 to 1904 he served as president of the National Geographic Society. To foster research in aviation, he put up money in 1907 for the Aerial Experiment Association; the group soon developed the hydrofoil speedboat and, in 1919, used it to set a world speed record of an astonishing 70 miles per hour. Bell died in Nova Scotia three years later.

Derby

The most famous of American horse races, the Churchill Downs extravaganza known as the Kentucky Derby, was named for and modeled on England's most famous race, the Epsom Downs event known simply as *the* Derby. That event was named for Edward Stanley, the twelfth earl of Derby (1752–1834), an avid amateur sportsman who in 1780 sponsored the first Epsom Downs run. The narrow-brimmed, bowl-shaped hat known as a *derby* was in turn named for the English race; it was first manufactured in the United States in the late nineteenth century, and was advertised as the kind of hat that was popular among viewers of the Derby.

The Stanley name is a distinguished one in English history. Edward's ancestor Thomas, the first earl, was the stepfather of Henry VII, the first Tudor king. The fourteenth earl, also named Edward, was prime minister three times in the mid-nineteenth century. The Stanley of equestrian fame was a lackluster *tertium quid* between these two celebrities. Educated at Eton and Cambridge, he entered Parliament in 1774 and was described by Horace Walpole as a competent speaker but also "a very raw, light, young man, given up to his pleasures." Those pleasures included, in addition to horse racing, cockfighting and the usual partying rounds of London society. Such entertainments sustained him through a long and forgettable career as lord lieutenant for his home county.

Stanley may have turned to the horses as a respite from a miserable private life. Four years after his marriage to the beautiful Elizabeth Hamilton (who was painted by Sir Joshua Reynolds), she left him for the duke of Dorset. He immediately had her portrait burned, and for the next twenty years steadfastly refused her a divorce to prevent her from marrying his rival. During this period he wooed the actress Elizabeth Farran, who evidently refused him her favors out of respect for his shattered but still legal union. The matter was settled in 1797, when the first Elizabeth died and Derby, six weeks later, began a long and amiable marriage with the second.

Derrick

In contemporary usage, a *derrick* is a structure supporting tackle, used either in construction (as in a movable or stationary crane) or in drilling (as in an oil well housing). Both these usages derive from an older sense of the word as a device on which not inanimate but human weight could be suspended: the original derricks were gallows. They were named for a seventeenth-century English executioner whose Christian name legend has misplaced, but whom the dramatist Thomas Dekker and others mention as the celebrity hangman of his day.

Derrick served under Elizabeth I's favorite courtier, the earl of Essex, in the 1596 expedition to Cadiz and, while there, was pardoned by the earl for a rape. Essex lived to regret his magnanimity. Five years later, foiled in a plot to unseat the queen's government, he became, on London's Tyburn hill, one of Derrick's most famous victims.

Dewey Decimal System

The American bibliophile Melvil Dewey (1851–1931) was the founder of library science in the United States. In 1876, his *annus mirabilis,* he not only created the book classification scheme that bears his name but also helped to found the American Library Association and became the first editor of *Library Journal*. Eleven years later, as librarian of Columbia College (later Columbia University), he gave his infant science academic respectability by establishing the country's first school of "library economy." Under Dewey's tutelage librarianship ceased to be a euphemism for book-watching and became an organized discipline.

An ardent defender of the metric system, Dewey based his classification apparatus on a division of knowledge into ten broad areas—subject classes 000 (generalities) through 500 (pure sciences) to 900 (geography and history)—all of which could be subdivided, depending on the complexity of the subject, out to several decimal places. For example, if you were seeking books on "working women," you would be directed by the card catalogue to the 331.4 section: 300 for social sciences, then 330 for economics, 331 for labor economics, and finally 331.4 for women workers. The more recent Library of Congress letter-and-number apparatus provides somewhat more flexibility for large collections, but Dewey's elegantly simple scheme is still favored by most school and public library systems.

Beginning in 1889, Dewey served in the library administration of his home state, New York. While there he shepherded into popularity one additional innovation: the traveling library, or "bookmobile," system that has been extending informal education to rural areas for nearly a century.

Diesel Engine

The German engineer Rudolf Diesel (1858–1913) designed the oil fuel engine that figures so prominently today in industry and transportation. Born in Paris, Diesel graduated at the head of his class from a Munich engineering school, then began a decade-long study of thermodynamics with the goal of producing a more efficient engine than the ones then in use. The result was the first practical engine (1897) that utilized air compression rather than electrical ignition to create internal combustion.

Internal-combustion engines are powered by a series of tiny explosions that drive the pistons in the piston cylinders. In the original internal combustion engines—those that Diesel knew in his youth and that power most of our automobiles today—the explosions are caused by electrical sparks that ignite the air and fuel mixture in the cylinder. Diesel, understanding that air temperature rises rapidly under compression, did away with the sparks. His 1892 patent describes a machine in which the required explosions occur as fuel is injected into the shaft at the instant of highest compression—and thus highest volatility.

Diesel was more engineer than merchandiser. His 1898 working model attracted some notice—American brewer Adolphus Busch, seeing the possibilities, quickly took over U.S. licensing—but the inventor was financially unstable until his death. This occurred on a Channel crossing, when he fell overboard and was drowned.

Dionysian

The ancient god Dionysus, imported into Greece probably from the orgiastic East, presided over the breaking of boundaries. A woodlands and wildlands deity, he was the youngest of the OLYMPIANS, the excessive counter (as Nietzsche knew) to the god of restraint and order, Apollo. The original *Dionysian* revelries were both unrestrained and deadly. Devotees of the god, universally female, would stalk through the vastness of northern Greece until they found a wild animal, preferably a goat. Taking this lucky creature as the god, they would tear it to pieces and devour it, in a primitive version of divine cannibalism that would lead, by the fifth century B.C., to Greek tragedy (that is, songs to the *tragos,* or goat, Dionysus), and eventually to the sanitized Christian Eucharist.

The women who thus ate their god were known as maenads (from which *maniac*) or bacchantes. Euripides made the bacchantes, or Bacchae, the subject of his most terrifying drama, in which the victim of maniac frenzy is King Pentheus. The Romans, more literal than the Greeks, transformed the amorphous wildcat Dionysus into the relatively sedate Bacchus, god of wine. Thus a *bacchanal* today has come to mean something on the order of *Animal House*—an opportunity for tipsy sophomores to dress up in togas and go wild.

Doily

The small, often lace, mat that today goes by the name of *doily* is the sole surviving reminder of a prosperous eighteenth-century textile merchant. According to a *Spectator* issue of 1712, Doily "raised a Fortune by finding out materials for such Stuffs as might at once be cheap and genteel." The owner of a linen shop in central London, he was particularly successful in marketing a lightweight summer fabric that became quickly known as Doily cloth. Another specialty was a fringed table napkin, the "Doily napkin," which was the precursor of today's simple mat.

Doozy

The great American luxury cars of the 1930s were the Pierce Arrow, the Packard, the Cadillac, the Cord, and the Duesenberg —the original doozy. The Duesenberg SJ model roadster had a 320-horsepower engine and could do 130 miles per hour; it was so exquisitely tooled, inside and out, that the diminutive *Duesey*, later *doozy*, quickly became a byword (often used sarcastically) for excellence.

The man behind this engineering and design marvel was the German-born manufacturer Frederick S. Duesenberg (1876–1932). He emigrated to Iowa as a boy, and as a young man operated a bicycle business; he also earned a reputation as a racer, with pedaling against horses his specialty. Around the turn of the century Duesenberg turned to automobiles, working in Midwest factories and supply houses while developing a prototype of the famous Duesenberg motor. With his brother August he patented this high-performance engine in 1913 and began installing it in racing cars, speedboats, and airplanes. Evidently the boats were *doozies* too: the brothers' Chicago factory supplied the Allied navies with motors for a hundred subchasers in World War I; and in a Lake Michigan trial, a Duesenberg-powered speedster became the first boat in the world to top the speed of one mile a minute.

Doppler Effect

If you have ever sat in a railway station as a whistling locomotive passed through, you have observed a common example of the *Doppler effect*. You'll recall that the pitch of the whistle rises as the train approaches the station and falls off in a characteristic whine as it moves away. The reason is that, as the source of sound moves toward you, the sound waves it emits are crowded together, so that you hear more of them in a short period of time than you would have if the train had been stationary: the result is higher wave frequency and a correspondingly higher pitch. The reverse happens as the source of sound recedes: the waves are farther apart as they reach you, and you hear a low-frequency sound. As long as the source of sound and the listener are in motion relative to each other, you'll observe this Doppler effect.

The effect works not just in sound but in anything transmitted in waves: the rule is that motion affects perceived wave frequency. The Austrian scientist who described the effect, Christian Johann Doppler (1803–53), observed it in light waves, as he studied the stars. In 1842 he predicted that the color of luminous bodies would change—that is, that the observed frequency of their light waves would change—as they moved in space relative to an earthbound observer. Modern measurements have proved his conjecture right; the "red shift" observed in distant galaxies is now explained as a special case of the Doppler effect, caused by the fact that those galaxies are moving away from the Earth. Because of its applicability to all wave motion, the Doppler effect has numerous practical implications, especially in navigation, astronomy, and radar detection. If you are ever stopped by a radar trap, you will have Christian Doppler to thank.

Draconian Justice

The Greek statesman Draco was *archon,* or chief magistrate, of Athens in 621 B.C. Before his rule, the state's "legal" system was dominated by arbitrary officials, blood feuds, and pressure from a rising middle class on the hereditary privileges of the aristocracy. Draco was in effect hired by the wealthy to protect their property rights, and this he attempted to do by codifying the laws: the result was what is often considered a halting step toward justice, Athens's first written constitution.

In abolishing the hazards of caprice, however, Draco introduced rigidity and punitive excess. He stipulated capital punishment for so many crimes that *draconian justice* came to stand as a synonym for legal repression. His code lasted only for a generation, when the *archon* Solon was called upon to revise it.

Dun

The conservative *Oxford English Dictionary* sees *dun,* in the sense of "to make repeated demands for money," as a probable variant of "din," meaning "to ring with sound" or "resound." That is a reasonable enough suggestion, given the impression a debtor might be expected to have of a voice continually asking for payment. A more colorful explanation, ignored by the *OED,* is given as gospel by the eighteenth-century antiquarian Frances Grose. In an 1811 redaction of his endlessly entertaining *Classical Dictionary of the Vulgar Tongue,* we find that "the true original meaning of the word, owes its birth to one Joe Dun, a famous bailiff of the town of Lincoln, so extremely active, and so dexterous in his business, that it became a proverb, when a man refused to pay, Why do not you *Dun* him? that is, Why do not you set Dun to arrest him?"

Grose identifies Joe Dun, and the usage, as dating from Henry VII's reign (1485–1509). Since Henry began his rule heavily in debt from the Wars of the Roses, it may safely be assumed that there was dunning going on at the time. But the *OED* does not find *dun* used in this sense until a century after Henry's death, and so the Joe Dun tale remains conjectural.

Dunce

It is a major irony of Western cultural history that the name of one of the greatest of medieval thinkers should now evoke images of laggard students, mental slowness, and *dunce caps*. The Scottish-born theologian John Duns Scotus (1265–1308) was second only to Thomas Aquinas in his influence on ecclesiastical philosophy, and though he is remembered today chiefly as an architect of the Immaculate Conception doctrine, he wrote and lectured extensively in his own day on all aspects of metaphysics, logic, and theology. The history of high medieval thought, in fact, could fairly be characterized as the debate between the Dominican Thomists and the followers of the Scottish "Subtle Doctor," who like him were Franciscans.

Ordained in 1291, Scotus taught at Oxford and Paris, becoming regent master of theology in the French capital in 1305. He spent the last year of his life in Cologne, and was buried in the Franciscan church there. The association of his name with stupidity came about long after his death, during the humanist Renaissance of the sixteenth century. At that time Scotist scholars, called Dunses in memory of their master, formed the major opposition against the "new learning" and were specifically opposed to the revival of classical texts. In consequence of their intransigence, *dunce* came to mean first an adherent of backwardness and sophistry, and ultimately a blockhead or fool.

Drinks: Name Your Poison

Although my *Old Mr. Boston DeLuxe Official Bartender's Guide* gives recipes for dozens of eponymous cocktails, only a snootful are still served today. I will leave to more earnest bibulophiles the task of tracking down the folks behind the Ethel Duffy, the Harry Lauder, and the Biffy and confine myself to those entries that can actually help you win bar bets. With thanks to Old Mr. Boston and to John Mariani's *Dictionary of American Food and Drink,* here they are in order, more or less, of descending current popularity:

First is the famed *Bloody Mary,* which the tad biased Smirnoff Vodka Company calls the "single most popular mixed drink" in America. As to who first put tomato juice and Worcestershire sauce into vodka, the experts disagree, although the consensual nod is to Fernand Petiot, bartender in the 1920s at Harry's New York Bar in Paris. Ernest Hemingway claimed to have introduced the drink into Hong Kong at the beginning of World War II; it may probably be safely assumed that, as an old Harry's regular, he borrowed the recipe from Petiot. Smirnoff, with tongue in cheek, backs Georgie Jessel, the comic they hired in the 1950s to tout the drink on an advertising tour.

Jessel claims he named the pick-me-up for an acquaintance who was brave enough to sample his prototype. Everybody else agrees the Mary in question was Mary Tudor (1516–58), the Catholic queen of England who earned the epithet *Bloody Mary* by killing an average of one Protestant a week throughout the five years of her reign. She is not to be confused with her half-cousin Mary Queen of Scots; and, although a drink with extra vodka is called a Very Bloody Mary and one without vodka a Virgin Mary, there is no basis for believing, as certain whimsical bibliologists have suggested, that tomato juice spiked with Scotch whisky was once called a Mary Queen of Scotch.

The most popular American "short" drink, the *martini,* also has an uncertain provenance. An obvious choice for the namesake is the Italian firm of Martini & Rossi, which was making vermouth in the 1820s. A less obvious candidate is Friedrich von Martini, a Swiss firearms inventor who supplied the British with Martini-Henry rifles after 1871; the drink, John Mariani points out, was said to have "the kick of a Martini." Booze buffs largely agree that the actual inventor of the drink was a San Francisco bartender named Jerry Thomas, whose 1862 recipe book, *The Bon Vivant's Companion,* contains a mixture of gin and vermouth which he labeled "The Martinez." He said he named it for a customer; some say what he meant was a customer on his way to the nearby *town* of Martinez.

The martini is traditionally served with a lemon twist or, more commonly, a green olive. When a pearl onion is used instead, the drink becomes known as a *Gibson,* after the American illustrator Charles Dana Gibson; he is supposed to have been served the original one olive-short day in New York. Gibson, of course, is best remembered for his elegantly drawn GIBSON GIRLS.

A drink now spreading from the Sun Belt throughout the states is the tartly chic *margarita,* that combination of tequila, lime juice, and Triple Sec which has been known to make macho men cry and turn Gibson girls into raving *toreras.* Again the origin is disputed. Mariani cites Marion Gorman and Felipe de Alba, authors of the 1976 *Tequila Book,* who mention five outstanding claims, two of them suitably eponymous. Los Angeles bartender Daniel Negrete says he invented the drink in Mexico in 1936, for a girlfriend named Margarita. And San Antonian Margarita Sames claims it was invented for her, in an Acapulco bar in the 1950s. Either story works, with some salt.

The *Harvey Wallbanger,* a recent addition to the Dutch courage armory, sounds like a one-liner's joke, but apparently there really was a Harvey. He was a 1960s surfer who, after a disappointing showing in a Manhattan Beach tournament, started downing these orange juice, vodka, and Galliano DOOZIES as if they held the secret to the perfect wave. The unsurprising result was a wipeout. The drinks, in Mariani's coy phrasing, "caused him to bang into the wall."

The *Tom Collins* is less seen than it used to be, although it remains the favored tall-drink-of-water for those who are not fond of water. It was consumed around the time of the Civil War under the name *John Collins,* reputedly the bartender who invented it. Nobody has tracked him down, but we do know his presumed kinsman Tom. At the turn of this century a John Collins was mixed with dry, Dutch-style gin; the Tom Collins used a sweeter gin, marketed under the brand name Old Tom.

Sweet or dry, a Collins includes gin, citrus juice, soda water, and sugar. Without the sugar it's a *rickey,* named for a Colonel (some say Joe) Rickey, a Kentuckian who at the turn of the century was a society lush in the nation's capital.

The rickey is not to be confused with the *mickey,* or *Mickey Finn*. Michael Finn, according to Herb Caen's 1935 history *Don't Call It Frisco,* was a shady San Francisco barkeep during that city's nineteenth-century boom. As inside man of a shanghai ring, he would drug already drunken sailors so they could be carted away without trouble. Ever after, serving a beverage designed to knock a customer out has been known as *slipping him a mickey*.

The *Manhattan* is a collective eponym twice removed. Mariani says this mixture of whiskey, vermouth, and bitters was first served at New York's Manhattan Club in 1874, at a banquet given by Winston Churchill's mother, Jennie. The club was named for the borough, and the borough for the Indian people who inhabited it just before the Dutch: the Algonquin-speaking Manhattes.

The *Rob Roy,* or "Scotch Manhattan," keeps alive the nickname of the outlaw Robert MacGregor (1671–1734), known as the Scottish Robin Hood. He battled for years with Highland barons and was immortalized in Sir Walter Scott's 1817 novel—which undoubtedly influenced the drink.

The *brandy Alexander* is widely conceded to have been named for Alexander the Great. Why is anybody's guess. He was a notorious two-fisted imbiber, and this quintessential "lady's drink"—a froth of brandy, crème de cacao, and cream—would hardly seem to be fitting for a red-blooded Macedonian male.

A few generics: The southern colonel's favorite sipping whiskey, *bourbon,* was named for Kentucky's Bourbon County, where some of the best is still made. The county was named for the Bourbons, the line of Gallic royalty whose extravagances helped cause the French Revolution.

Grog, the sailor's term for rum and water, comes from the name of the British admiral who first had the sobering idea of diluting his crew's spirit rations. Edward Vernon (1684–1757) habitually wore a coat made of a coarse silk fabric known as grogram. Hence his nickname "Old Grog," *grog* as the slang term for unbuttered rum, and the adjective *groggy*. George Washington's brother once served under the admiral, and Mount Vernon is named in his honor.

Booze, meaning any hard liquor, is frequently associated with a Colonel Booze, an early nineteenth-century distiller who used bottles shaped like log cabins. The word actually dates back to Middle English *bouse,* "to drink," but clearly the colonel's marketing gimmick did help to popularize the usage.

If booze is in doubt, not so *hooch*. It dates back to the Klondike Gold Rush, during which a tribe of Alaskan Indians, the Hoochinoo, used to brew a mixture of yeast, flour, and molasses that gave real meaning to the term "firewater." It was so popular with the miners that the Dawson *Nugget* in 1898 called it that "joy-dispensing hooch."

Last, and certainly least, the *Shirley Temple*. Named for the curly-topped *Wunderkind* of the 1930s, it consists of 7-Up or ginger ale with a splash of grenadine. The height of sophisticated innocence, just like Shirley, it is of enormous value as a fidget-suppressant when one is between restaurant courses with children.

E

Echo

In Greek mythology, Echo was a gabby wood nymph whose loquaciousness proved her undoing at the hand of jealous Hera. Hera's spouse, the notoriously philandering Zeus, was frequently involved in trysts with the nymphs, and his wife's attempts to disclose his infidelities were often thwarted because she was distracted by Echo's constant chatter. Eventually she took revenge on the unwitting accomplice by depriving her of the power of speech—with the dubiously meliorating proviso that she would still be able to repeat the last words anyone said to her.

As if this were not enough for poor Echo, she subsequently fell in love with NARCISSUS, the handsome lad who scorned all who loved him. When he rejected her, she gradually wasted away, hiding in caves and wild places, until there was nothing left of her but her voice. In this rustic exile, perhaps, she met Pan (see PANIC); legend says that by him she had a daughter, Iynx. Iynx fared no better than her mother. Suspected by Hera of playing the matchmaker for Zeus and the priestess Io, she was transformed into a woodpecker.

Eiffel Tower

The Eiffel Tower means Paris as surely as BIG BEN means London. The imposing latticework structure was built for the 1889 Paris

Exposition by one of France's leading authorities on iron construction, the engineer Alexandre Gustave Eiffel (1832–1923). Educated as a chemical engineer, Eiffel formed a construction company in 1867 and quickly earned a reputation for doing sturdy large-scale work, especially railway spans, not only in Europe but as far afield as Russia and Latin America. In 1885 Eiffel's firm did the steel framework for Frederic Bartholdi's Statue of Liberty, and four years later came the government contract for the Left Bank landmark.

When it was erected, the Eiffel Tower, at 986 feet, was the tallest "building" in the world, and it retained that distinction until 1930, when New York's Chrysler Building topped it by sixty feet. Eiffel continued to work with tall buildings, and studied the aerodynamics of high frames so extensively that in the process he became an expert on meteorology. Many of the principles set out in his major book, *The Resistance of the Air and Aviation,* are still observed in skyscraper design.

Electra Complex

In the retrospective outline of his work that he wrote several months before he died, Sigmund Freud spoke of a feminine OEDIPUS COMPLEX which, like the more celebrated male variety, defined all psychological development as the result of early genital confusions. For a boy, Freud said, the intense attraction to the mother ends when he realizes that sleeping with her will lead to castration. For a girl, it is the belief that she has *already* been castrated which turns her from the mother and toward the father: resenting her mother because she has failed to provide her with a penis, she becomes Daddy's girl, first so she can "have his penis at her command" and then in the hope that he will give her a baby as a present. The entire complex of feminine psychology, including women's desire for marriage and motherhood, grows out of this perceived "loss" of a penis.

The "penis envy" scenario is often called the *Electra complex* because in Greek mythology Electra, in a reversal of the Oedipal design, is supposed to have killed her mother, Clytemnestra, out of love for her father. Actually, it's her brother Orestes who does the deed, although at Electra's instigation. Those who spy deep psychological significance in this story should remember that it is not an isolated incident, but only one act of a long bloody history. It begins with the sacrifice of Orestes' and Electra's sister Iphigenia by their father, Agamemnon. Next is the murder of Agamemnon by Clytemnestra, as a payment for her daughter's fate. Finally comes "Electra's" revenge. Considering the roles of Orestes and Iphigenia, any psychologist ought to be able to interpret this mess as a prototype of necrophilia or of "sister envy." That would be silly, of course, but it would have no less justification than the Freudian fairy tale.

A host of post-Freudian analysts have questioned the logic of the Electra complex theory, and feminists continually point out that penis envy is a masculine fantasy which serves to reflect, and reinforce, male CHAUVINISM. The social implications of the theory were brilliantly lampooned a few years ago by Gloria Steinem in *Ms.* magazine. Asking the rhetorical question of what would happen if men could menstruate, she answered: "Menstruation would become an enviable, boast-worthy, masculine event. Men would brag about how long and how much." And penis envy would give way to womb envy.

Epicure

Epicurus (341–270 B.C.) was an influential Greek philosopher whose namesakes *epicure* and *epicurean* suggest a devotion to sensual delights, especially those of the table. A typical epicurean existence, it is often supposed, revolves around wine, women, and twenty-course meals.

This would have come as quite a surprise to Epicurus. It is true that, as an early materialist, he said the universe could only be understood by a strict reliance on the senses. It is also true that he believed the only goal of human life should be pleasure. But he did not mean the wayward pleasures of the flesh. Epicurus defined pleasure as the absence of pain, and he counseled that the highest of all pleasures was that serene impassiveness the Greeks called *ataraxia*. This supreme goal was to be achieved, moreover, by the lessening, not the heightening, of desire.

It was unsympathetic commentators on Epicurus's teachings who transformed him into a patron of refined gluttony. Perhaps they resented his atheism, or the discomforting fact that his school at Athens, known as the Garden, accepted both slaves and women as students. In any event, the original Epicureans were much closer in nature to the STOICS than to the LUCULLAN Diamond Jim Brady.

Erotic

The adjective *erotic* comes from Eros, the ever young Greek god of love. Ancient writers differ on his origins. Some call him the oldest of the deities, a creature born of Chaos or of Night, who set the entire world in motion. Others say his mother was Aphrodite and his father either Mars, Mercury, or Zeus (see APHRODISIAL, MARTIAL, MERCURIAL). Perhaps the confusion about his origins reflects the Greeks' ambivalence about the erotic: certainly the recklessness with which Eros inspired passion hints at the destructive as well as the joyous nature of desire. This becomes even more evident in the Roman period, when Eros's counterpart Cupid is typically depicted as a mischievous (and often blindfolded) child, randomly shooting his arrows with no thought of consequence or design. It is left to relatively modern times to turn this high-spirited brat into the romanticized cherub seen on VALENTINES. Cupid, of course, gives us *cupidity*, implying avarice as well as desire.

Eustachian Tube

In the sixteenth-century debate between followers of the ancient Greek physician Galen and proponents of the "new anatomy," Bartolomeo Eustachius (ca. 1520–74) began on the reactionary side, championing Galen, who had extrapolated from animal anatomy, against such revolutionaries as Andreas Vesalius and Gabriel Fallopius (see FALLOPIAN TUBES), who were dissecting human corpses. Forced to adopt their observational techniques in order to refute them, however, he was converted to the new scientific method and subsequently undertook investigations that were decidedly Vesalian in approach. His study *Opuscula Anatomica* (1564) contained essays on the veins, kidneys, teeth, and ears; in the last, he identified the canal which connects the middle ear to the back of the throat, thus equalizing pressure on the eardrum. It was named the *eustachian tube* in his honor.

Born in San Severino, about fifty miles south of Urbino, Eustachius was for a time personal physician to the important Renaissance art patron, the duke of Urbino; he later attended a Roman cardinal. His anatomical work apparently was less appreciated in his day than it might have been; the illustrations to his major work, *Tabulae Anatomicae,* were not published until 1714.

F

Fahrenheit Scale

Gabriel Daniel Fahrenheit (1686–1736) developed the first practical mercury thermometer around 1720 and assigned it the measurement scale that still bears his name. Fahrenheit took the freezing and boiling temperatures of water as the scale's basic "end points," and chose as an internal fixed point the "body temperature" of 96 degrees. With this point recalculated later as 98.6, and with the upper and lower points set at 212 degrees and 32 degrees, Fahrenheit's system soon became standard in Holland and the English-speaking countries. Even today it remains far more widely used in the United States, except for scientific purposes, than the simpler CELSIUS scale.

Born in Germany, Fahrenheit wandered widely through Europe as a young man, studying the methods of fellow amateur scientists. Settling in Amsterdam in 1717, he manufactured scientific instruments and in spite of his lack of formal education became widely respected in the academic community: four years after introducing his most famous invention, he was admitted to the Royal Academy. Among his other contributions were a pumping device for draining the Dutch polders and a hygrometer, for measuring atmospheric humidity.

Fallopian Tubes

The *fallopian tubes,* which carry eggs from the ovaries to the uterus, were discovered by and named after the Italian anatomist Gabriel Fallopius (1523–62). A friend and colleague of Vesalius, he joined with him in rejecting the speculative bias of classical science and replacing it with meticulous observation based on the dissection of corpses. As professor of surgery and anatomy first at Pisa and then at Vesalius's own university, Padua, Fallopius performed extensive studies of the cranial nerves, genital organs, and inner ear: our terms "palate," "placenta," "cochlea," "clitoris," and "vagina" all were first proposed by him. Although less revolutionary a work than Vesalius's 1543 anatomy, his *Observationes Anatomicae* (1561) was still a milestone in Renaissance research.

Faustian

The Western concept of progress is fueled by two intermingled cultural dispositions: the restless yearning for new experiences and the perilous Adamic fantasy of exerting mastery over nature through knowledge. Both these elements are displayed forcefully in the late medieval Faust legend, and it is because of that legend that *Faustian* means both "insatiable" and "damned."

The original Johann (or Georg) Faustus was a wandering German necromancer who lived at the beginning of the sixteenth century. His supposed magical powers and boastful charm made him the subject of many stories, and these were collected after his death in a series of popular Faustbooks. The first major treatment of the legend, Christopher Marlowe's 1588 play *Dr. Faustus,* established the hero as a tragic figure, losing his soul to the Devil as the price for attaining worldly knowledge. Marlowe's basic plot outline, in which power implies a pact with the Devil, proved extremely fertile ground for future artists. Goethe's masterly two-part drama *Faust* (1808 and 1832) enshrined the peculiarly Western idea of striving *(Streben)* as the central, awful beauty of human life. Gounod and Berlioz wrote operas on the theme, and in 1947, just after human intelligence had created World War II and the Bomb, Thomas Mann made the legendary striver a kind of shadow model for the hero of his dark masterpiece *Doctor Faustus*.

Ferris Wheel

As chief architectural planner for the 1893 World's Columbian Exposition in Chicago, Daniel H. Burnham was eager to showcase American talent, and in particular to produce a homegrown structure that would rival the EIFFEL TOWER, which had GALVANIZED Paris four years earlier. Virtually every major architect in the country contributed to Burnham's "White City," but the structure that drew the crowds and came to symbolize American ingenuity was an upright rotating wheel 250 feet in diameter with hanging cars for passengers. It was created by a civil engineer named George Washington Gale Ferris.

Born in Illinois in 1859, Ferris was the son of George Washington Ferris and Martha Ferris—a propitious start for a young man who would grow up to celebrate American genius. Educated at Rensselaer Polytechnic Institute, he worked in the 1880s on the standard engineering tasks: building railroads, bridges, and tunnels. A pioneer in the use of structural steel, he also foresaw the need for proper inspection of newly milled steel, and in Pittsburgh he founded a company that conducted on-site testing throughout the nation. At the time of the Exposition, he was engaged in building a series of bridges across the Ohio River.

Ferris's original wheel was capable of carrying over 2,000 passengers at one time in its thirty-six cars. An enormous success, it fostered many imitators at the turn of the century, the most notable being a 300-foot wheel constructed for the 1897 London fair and a 197-foot one built for Vienna's Prater Park in 1896; the Vienna creation is the largest Ferris wheel still in operation. These fin-de-siècle giants proved impractical, of course, for the many carnival midways where Ferris's invention now prospers: the average traveling wheel today is about 50 feet in diameter.

After the Exposition closed, Ferris returned to his bridge-building and steel-testing businesses until his untimely death in

1896. Eight years later the structure that had started the craze, built at a cost of $385,000, was sold for scrap in St. Louis. It fetched less than $2,000.

Fink

A *fink* is either an informer or a strikebreaker; whichever meaning is intended, the implication is that the fink prefers to side with "Authority" and thus betray the interests of the "People." The word is the shortest explosion I know of the myth that America is a classless society.

As a synonym for "stoolie" or "snitch," the term is probably a contraction for "finger." As a synonym for "blackleg" or "scab," its derivation is less certain. The most plausible explanation I have encountered is H. L. Mencken's suggestion that it arose in the infamous Homestead strike of 1892, when the management of the Carnegie Steel Company plant in Homestead, Pennsylvania, cut workers' wages, locked out those who responded by striking, and then brought in Pinkerton Agency detectives to run things until the strike was broken. These detectives were known first as *Pinks,* and ultimately as *finks*.

Homestead was only one of many places where the Pinkertons were enlisted against workers. Founded by Scottish immigrant Allan Pinkerton (1819–84) in 1850 to investigate railroad theft, the agency eventually evolved into a kind of industrial shock battalion, primed to squash labor unrest. The Pinks' effectiveness at Homestead, and later in the PULLMAN strike, provided serious setbacks in the 1890s to the fledgling unionism movement.

Frankenstein

On vacation in Italy in 1816, the English poet Lord Byron suggested a storytelling contest to some friends. The friends were the poet Percy Bysshe Shelley, his writer wife, Mary Shelley, and Byron's physician, a Dr. Polidori. The proposed subject of the contest was ghosts. Mary Shelley's entry was *Frankenstein,* the now classic tale of scientific hubris in which a student makes a monster out of corpses and is ultimately destroyed by his creation. In Shelley's story, published in 1818 as *Frankenstein, or the Modern Prometheus,* "Frankenstein" meant the student, Victor Frankenstein; since about 1840, the term has been applied to the monster, so that we refer, bluntly but incorrectly, to a creation that has escaped our control as "a Frankenstein."

Mary Shelley (1797–1851) was the daughter of English radicals William Godwin and Mary Wollstonecraft, and her novel is burdened with turgidities about the origin of evil. Its queer focus on creativity and human yearning, however, captured the romantic imagination, and the more lurid aspects of the tale have made it a staple of gothic melodrama. The 1931 Universal film version established the "mad scientist" movie motif and made Boris Karloff a star. Of its numerous ludicrous imitations, the worst is probably the 1966 *Jesse James Meets Frankenstein's Daughter.*

Freudian Slip

Nothing better illustrates Sigmund Freud's commitment to the hidden meaning than his thinking on slips of the tongue. The founder of psychoanalysis first wrote on these common "parapraxes" shortly after the publication of his pioneering *Interpretation of Dreams* (1901), which presented his early ideas on the unconscious, repression, and the sexually active infantile mind. In 1904 his essay on verbal slips appeared as Chapter 5 of his most popular book, *The Psychopathology of Everyday Life.* It was that book that made every sophomore in Europe and America an instant armchair expert on the mind and led to the cant term *Freudian slip* to describe any and all verbal errors, whatever their gravity or content. Before Freud, slips of the tongue were meaningless errors; now even the most innocent mistake takes on a deep, forbidding significance.

Freudophiles without the master's clinical background or knowledge of languages have given his kind of linguistic analysis a bad name, but that should not obscure Freud's contribution to our understanding of "meaningless" utterances. In his essay and throughout later lectures, he gave numerous examples of slips that hinted at what he called the secondary process of mental functioning. If his followers gave the world the idea that every such error was "Freudian"—and that Freudian meant "Sex is all that counts"—that was their problem, not his. Many of the examples in *Psychopathology,* in fact, have nothing to do with the EROTIC: Consider the woman who describes her soldier son as being with the "42nd Murderers" instead of "Mortars," or the dentist who reveals his mercenary interest in his patients by replacing the dental term *Kontakt* (contact between teeth) with the unintentional *Kontant* (money). Freud was better aware than his followers that, to quote a joke often attributed to him, sometimes a cigar is "just a cigar."

Man Friday

"Man Friday," for a loyal and resourceful assistant, comes from Daniel Defoe's first novel, *Robinson Crusoe* (1719), in which the shipwrecked hero Crusoe rescues and befriends a young savage, then gives him the English name Friday for the day on which they first met. *Robinson Crusoe* blended elements of the then fashionable travel narrative (it was based on the story of Scottish castaway Alexander Selkirk) with a staunchly middle-class commitment to industry, self-reliance, and faith in providence. As popular in its own day as in ours, it made Defoe, at the age of fifty-nine, his country's first best-selling novelist.

A first-rate political satirist, Defoe (1660–1731) began his literary career as a pamphleteer and was imprisoned in 1702 for attacking government checks on religious freedom. For a decade he wrote the one-man *Review,* a journal of political economy, while serving as a writer and sometime secret agent for the speaker of the House of Commons. His 1706 report on "Mrs. Veal"—a woman who had supposedly returned from the dead in 1705—has been called the first ghost story written in English, and his *Journal of the Plague Year* realistically evokes the bubonic pestilence that devastated England when he was five. Defoe's grasp of realism, social forces, and human character is also effectively displayed in his second great contribution to the English novel, his history of the "fallen woman" *Moll Flanders*.

Frisbee

According to information kindly sent me by the Wham-O company of San Gabriel, California, the Frisbee was named after the Frisbie Pie Company, founded in Bridgeport, Connecticut, in 1871 by William Russell Frisbie. With his sister Susan, Frisbie managed the bakery into a highly successful enterprise, ultimately reaching pie-lovers as far away as Providence and Poughkeepsie. W. R. died in 1903, just about the time that Yale students in nearby New Haven discovered that the tins in which his wares were baked and shipped made excellent flying saucers. Thus the prototype "Frisbie" was born.

Frisbee fanciers were confined to the metallic form of the disc until 1948, when a West Coast inventor named Fred Morrison, capitalizing on the postwar fascination with UFOs, started manufacturing something called Morrison's Flyin' Saucer—the original plastic Frisbee. He hawked this gismo on street corners for the next seven years. In 1955, a couple of young entrepreneurs, Rich Knerr and A. K. Melin, picked up on the idea. Two years later, their Wham-O company started its production line, calling their new product the *Frisbee* simply because Knerr had heard some college students use the term; he had never heard of the Bridgeport pie company.

Since that first unit rolled off the line, over 100 million Frisbees have been sold, and, throwing has become highly sophisticated and competitive. Little did Susan and W. R. realize that they were baking up a national obsession.

On the Fritz

Although the standard etymological sources come up dry on the origin of this synonym for "on the blink" or "broken," William and Mary Morris, authors of the *Dictionary of Word and Phrase Origins,* offer a plausible explanation. The original Fritz, they suggest, was one of the "Katzenjammer Kids"—a scamp who, with his twin brother, Hans, made a popular comic strip career out of sabotaging parental "law and order."

Like PECK'S BAD BOY of the 1880s and Dennis the Menace of this century, Hans and Fritz Katzenjammer were cutups with hearts of gold. Created by graphic artist Rudolph Dirks in 1897, they can fairly lay claim to being, in the words of Maurice Horn, the protagonists of "the oldest comic strip in existence." Against their foils, "die Mama," "der Inspector," and "der Captain," they perpetrated every schoolboy prank ever thought of, and managed to make pidgin German as ready a spur to light-hearted xenophobia as "Chinee talk" had been a decade before, or as the Polish joke would become in the 1960s.

With the advent of World War I, the *Katzenjammer Kids,* drawn by new artist Harold Knerr, changed its name to *Shenanigan Kids*. It changed back in 1919, and the strip continued to be carried by American papers well into the middle of this century.

Fudge

As a noun, *fudge* is a candy. As an exclamation it approximates "Oh, darn!" As a verb it suggests falsification, as of test results, materials, or resumes. In this last sense it has frequently been associated with a mendacious seventeenth-century sea captain named "Lying" Fudge; no less an authority than Isaac D'Israeli, father of the British prime minister, remarked (in his *Curiosities of Literature*) that this Captain Fudge was the namesake for the nautical expression "You fudge it!" as an equivalent for "You lie." The *Oxford English Dictionary* mocks this tale, though there is modest circumstantial evidence to support it: the first appearance of the slang term in print was in a 1674 treatise on shipping. While admitting that the captain was real, the *OED* hints that this entry may itself have been a misprint, or a fudge.

Fu Manchu Mustache

A heavy mustache that turns down toward the chin at the ends is called a *Fu Manchu* after the sinister, mustachioed title character of the 1913 English novel *Dr. Fu Manchu.* The author was a Birmingham-born journalist named Arthur Wade (or Ward), born around 1883, who combined an interest in the occult with an acquaintance with London's Chinese criminals to create a memorable personal version of the inscrutable Oriental: his doctor, a malevolent genius surrounded by mindless henchmen, was the Yellow Peril in the flesh.

Dr. Fu Manchu, published under the pseudonym Sax Rohmer, was the initial effort of a writer who produced almost fifty novels before his death, including a dozen more starring the evil doctor. Picked up by both American and British filmmakers, the Fu Manchu vogue hit its peak in the 1930s, with Boris Karloff's 1932 characterization in *The Mask of Fu Manchu* being the high point of five Hollywood versions. After World War II, with the xenophobia of the interwar years somewhat softened, Fu Manchu's popularity waned, although he was briefly reborn in a series of 1960s potboilers with the British horror darling Christopher Lee. Rohmer wrote his last novel, *Reenter Fu Manchu,* in 1957, and died two years later.

Food: They Were What You Eat

Many of our traditional foods are eponymous but also anonymous. We know nothing of the original apple Betty, for example. If there was a real Sloppy Joe, his history has not been written; nor has that of the itinerant Irish adventurer who gave us that hobo's delight, Mulligan Stew. Was there a Jack behind the flapjack? And who was the unsung Charles for whom the most "affordable" cut of beef is called "chuck"?

Some gastronomic gifts, however, have preserved the histories of their makers. Herewith a handful of my favorites, gleaned largely from John Mariani's stimulating *Dictionary of American Food and Drink*.

Fettuccine Alfredo

This light but hearty dish—fettuccine in a butter, cream, and Parmesan cheese sauce—was created in 1920 by Roman restaurant owner Alfredo di Lellio. It was popularized in the United States by the Earl Wilsons of the day, who pointed out to movie fans that, on their honeymoon in the Eternal City, Douglas Fairbanks and Mary Pickford patronized Alfredo's every day.

Eggs Benedict

Authorities agree that *eggs Benedict*—English muffins topped with ham or Canadian bacon, poached eggs, and hollandaise sauce—

were created by a New York city chef for a customer named Benedict. After that they diverge. One story gives the restaurant as Delmonico's and the patrons as a Mr. and Mrs. Le Grand Benedict, who were simply in the mood for something new. Another, more colorful tale says the Waldorf-Astoria's famous chef Oscar Tschirky invented the dish around the turn of the century for a hung-over lounge lizard named Samuel Benedict. Why he thought hollandaise sauce would snap him out of it is anybody's guess.

Caesar Salad

An Italian-American chef named Caesar Cardini, who opened a string of restaurants in Tijuana between the wars, created the salad that bears his name in 1924. His ingredients were romaine lettuce, garlic, olive oil, Worcestershire sauce, Parmesan cheese, croutons, and a coddled egg. The anchovies that appear in modern Caesar salads he considered a perversion. His original recipe, *sans anchois,* is still marketed today by Caesar Cardini Foods of Culver City, California.

Chateaubriand

The Vicomte François René de Chateaubriand (1768–1848) wrote melancholic romantic novels, travel narratives, and tracts against the French Revolution. The tenderloin cut named for him—generally served with mushrooms and béarnaise sauce—was invented, according to the juiciest story, by an unknown Parisian chef on a night when the writer's dinner guest was the celebrated gastronome Anthelme Brillat-Savarin.

Dagwood Sandwich

To make a *Dagwood sandwich,* you simply place the entire contents of your refrigerator between two slices of bread. The originator of this mile-high heartburn special "snack" was the comic strip character Dagwood Bumstead, the pleasantly ineffectual husband of perky, level-headed Blondie. The *Blondie* strip was created by cartoonist Chic Young (1901–73) in 1930; Dagwood came on board three years later.

Graham Cracker

Sylvester Graham (1794–1851) led a temperance and diet reform movement in the 1830s that brought thousands of people into cold-turkey-cure "boardinghouses" and that attracted such eminent Americans as Amelia Jenks BLOOMER, William Lloyd Garrison, and Horace Greeley. Graham's puritanical zeal was directed against meat, the demon rum, sexual excess—and white bread. The bran-rich wheat flour he championed was used to make "Graham bread" and later "Graham crackers." In his excellent study *Sex, Diet, and Debility in Jacksonian America,* historian Stephen Nissenbaum points out that the first commercial *graham crackers* were manufactured by a one-time Graham disciple, the popular "water cure" physician Russell Trall.

K Rations

The World War II serviceman's nutritionally correct, if uninspiring, packets of field food were designed by Minnesota physiologist Ancel Keys (1904–). Keys has received far more kudos from his professional colleagues than he ever did from G. I. Joe. A recipient of doctorates from the University of California and Cambridge, he has worked for the Mayo Foundation since 1936 and is now emeritus professor of physiological hygiene at the University of Minnesota.

Chicken à la King

Diced chicken in a cream and sherry sauce, this dish was originally chicken à la Keene, and only later corrupted to suggest a royal provenance. London's Claridge's Hotel claimed that the Keene in question was equestrian J. R. Keene and said its chef had created the dish to memorialize his 1881 Grand Prix victory. Others say J. R.'s son Foxhall, the self-styled "world's greatest amateur athlete," suggested the recipe to the chef at New York's Delmonico's.

Mayonnaise

This originally French, and now thoroughly Americanized, dressing may have been named, distantly, after Mago, brother of the Carthaginian general Hannibal, who threatened Rome in the second Punic War. The port city of Mahon, in Minorca, was originally Portus Magonis (Mago's Port), and the story goes that when Richelieu briefly captured it from the English in 1762, his chefs memorialized the occasion by creating "mahonnaise." The *Larousse Gastronomique* settles for a more mundane explanation: the word derives from Old French *moyeu,* for "egg yolk."

Melba Toast

One of the great divas of the nineteenth century, the coloratura soprano Helen Mitchell (1859–1931) took the stage name Nellie Melba in honor of her hometown, Melbourne, Australia. Her popularity on the London stage led to her being made a Dame of the British Empire, and to a pair of gastronomic innovations: the dieter's delight *melba toast* and the dieter's bane *peach melba* (peaches, ice cream, and raspberry sauce). Both were supposedly devised for the chronically overweight prima donna by noted chef Georges Escoffier.

Lobster Newburg

Lobster in a cream and sherry sauce was popularized at Delmonico's toward the end of the last century. The original name was lobster Wenberg, after a seagoing patron who had brought the recipe to New York from the Caribbean. This Wenberg (Charles or Ben, depending on your source) later wore out his welcome by making a drunken scene in the restaurant's main dining room; the next day the irate owner altered the menu title to *Newburg*. Robert Hendrickson suggests the change may also have been a nod to the upper Hudson River city of Newburgh, Washington's headquarters for a year during the Revolution.

Reuben Sandwich

Most of this sandwich's many admirers would agree that its basic ingredients are corned beef, rye bread, sauerkraut, and Russian dressing; revisionists add Swiss cheese and/or mustard. *Time* magazine, in a June 16, 1986, story, makes two plausible guesses at its creator. The Reuben was invented either by Omaha grocer Reuben Kay as a treat for his poker pals or by New York deli owner Arnold Reuben, who was famous in the 1940s and 1950s for naming his innovative sandwiches after celebrities.

Salisbury Steak

Everyone who has ever ordered Salisbury "steak" and been served a hamburger drenched in brown gravy has James H. Salisbury to thank. An English physician in the 1880s, Salisbury promoted a diet that would have given Sylvester GRAHAM nightmares: it called for ground beef three times a day. Among the ailments that this cholesterol-lover's regimen was supposed to cure were hardening of the arteries and colitis—two little devils we now know love nothing so much as red meat.

Sandwich

John Montagu, the fourth earl of Sandwich (1718–92), did not actually invent the snack for which he is famous, although he certainly consumed his share. A career politician, he was first lord of the admiralty in North's administration and also a notorious lecher and gambler. During one of his all-day gaming sessions, the legend goes, rather than leave the table to eat he ordered a servant to bring him an impromptu meal of roast beef between slices of bread: thus our term *sandwich* was born.

Beef Stroganoff

This exquisite blend of sliced beef, mushrooms, and sour cream immortalizes Paul Stroganoff, a nineteenth-century Russian nobleman and diplomat inordinately fond of the dish. As far as Mother Russia is concerned, it is his only memorial: the mammoth *Great Soviet Encyclopedia* gives the czarist functionary not a nod.

Beef Wellington

The pièce de résistance of many a posh establishment, beef Wellington is a cut of prime beef wrapped in bacon and pâté and then cooked in a puff pastry shell. It was named for Great Britain's Iron Duke, Napoleon's undoing at Waterloo, Arthur Wellesley, the first duke of Wellington (1769–1852). Soon after his famous victory, his name was also attached to various articles of clothing, notably the *Wellington overcoat* and the fashionable dragoon-style boots called simply WELLINGTONS.

In case you're not full yet, here's a selection of eponymous candy for dessert:

Baby Ruth

Mariani cites the common story that it was named for President Grover Cleveland's daughter. An equally feasible choice (see my *Fabulous Fallacies*) is the granddaughter of George Williamson, president of the company that introduced the bar in 1920.

Hershey Bar

The brainchild and first great success of chocolate king Milton S. Hershey (1857–1945), the Hershey bar was introduced in 1894. Milton followed it with the equally successful Hershey's Kisses in 1907.

Oh Henry!

Introduced by George Williamson's company a year after the Baby Ruth, it was named not after the writer O. Henry but after a young gofer named Henry. Requests like "Oh, Henry, would you get me another barrel of peanuts?" were heard so often around the factory that the new peanut bar was named in his honor.

Reese's Peanut Butter Cups

Another staple of the Hershey empire, they were named after their inventor, Hershey employee H. B. Reese, who started his own plant in 1923 and merged back with the parent concern forty years later. H. B. also gave his name to Reese's Pieces, the candy favored by the eponymous hero of the blockbuster movie *E.T.*

Three Musketeers

Manufactured by the Mars Company since 1932, this bar was named after Alexandre Dumas's 1844 novel and was originally packaged in three sections, corresponding presumably to the Aramis, Athos, and Porthos of the story.

Tootsie Roll

Introduced in 1896, it was named by its creator, Leo Hirschfield, after his daughter Clara, whom he affectionately called "Tootsie." The Tootsie Roll Pop followed in 1930.

* * *

Finally, for those with more continental tastes, there is the sugarmaniac's ultimate treat, the deadly *praline*. The French *pralin* is composed of sugar and caramelized almonds, and was named for César du Plessis-Praslin (1598–1675), once minister of state to Louis XIV. The American version, introduced through New Orleans, substitutes pecans for the almonds.

G

Gallup Polls

The *Gallup polls* are not only the best recognized but also the oldest surviving American opinion surveys. They are named for George H. Gallup (1901–84), the journalist and advertising executive who conceived the idea for such national pulse-taking in 1935.

Born in Iowa, Gallup took a doctorate in journalism from the state university in 1928, with a thesis on reader interest in newspapers. In the early 1930s he taught journalism and conducted reader-interest surveys for midwestern newspapers. One result of his findings was that the Des Moines *Register and Tribune* company, responding to public interest in photography, began to publish *Look* magazine. In 1932 he began what was to be a fifteen-year association with the advertising firm of Young and Rubicam, where he applied his survey principles to market research.

In 1935, on the eve of the presidential election, Gallup formed the American Institute of Public Opinion "to measure and report public opinion on political and social issues of the day without regard to the rightness or wisdom of the views expressed." The Institute's prediction of Roosevelt's victory over Alf Landon brought Gallup and his polling group into the public eye. In spite of subsequent lapses in accuracy (the poll predicted Dewey in 1948, for example), it has remained there ever since.

In 1958 Gallup established the Gallup Organization to conduct independent market research; he also founded Quill and Scroll, the high-school journalism honor society. Sensitive to the criticism that his surveys often created a bandwagon effect, he consistently defended the public opinion poll as a check against lobbies and pressure groups, and in his best-received book, *The Pulse of Democracy* (1940), called it "an instrument for improving self-government."

Galvanize

To *galvanize,* in the sense of "to stimulate" or "to excite," comes to us courtesy of Luigi Galvani (1737–98), an Italian physiologist whose work on muscular response laid the groundwork for modern electrophysiology. Born in Bologna, Galvani taught anatomy at the university there from 1762, and in 1780 began experimenting on frogs to prove a theory of "animal electricity." Linking his subjects by brass hooks to an iron railing, he observed continual muscle contractions, which he took to be evidence of an electrical "fluid" within the animals' bodies. This conclusion was later disproven by Alessandro Volta (see VOLT), who showed that the electrical discharge originated outside the frogs, from the contact between the hooks and the railing.

Although his theory was invalidated, Galvani's name has survived. In addition to *galvanize* in the broad sense indicated above, we have *galvanized iron or steel* (metal that has been "electrochemically" coated with zinc); the *galvanometer,* for measuring electrical current; and the *galvanic skin response* (GSR), the change in electrical resistance of the skin which is the basis of polygraph testing.

Gargantuan

Gargantua is the giant, gluttonous protagonist of François Rabelais's lusty novel *Gargantua and Pantagruel.* The Renaissance, aware of the word's derivation (*garganta* in Spanish is "throat"), commonly used *gargantuan* to describe a prodigious appetite. In *As You Like It,* for example, when Rosalind rattles off ten quick questions and finishes with "Answer me in one word," Shakespeare has Celia respond: "You must borrow me Gargantua's mouth first: 'tis a word too great for any mouth of this age's size." The contemporary meaning is broader: almost anything of great size may, in legitimate slang, be depicted today as *gargantuan.*

Rabelais (1494?–1553) was a French scholar, monk, and physician whose comic satire, appearing in five books between 1532 and 1564, had an obvious influence on such Enlightenment picaresques as *Gulliver's Travels* and *Candide.* Because of his boisterous irreverence toward social and religious conventions, we use the adjective *Rabelaisian* to mean licentious, extravagant, or merely coarse.

Geiger Counter

The German physicist Hans Wilhelm Geiger invented various instruments for measuring the rate of radioactive emissions; the one that bears his name, developed in the 1920s by Geiger and his colleague Wilhelm Müller, remains in universal use in industrial, laboratory, and mining applications.

Born in the Rheinland in 1882, Geiger received his doctorate from Erlangen in 1906, worked in England for several years with Ernest Rutherford, and in 1912 became director of a radium research laboratory in Berlin. In the 1920s he taught physics at Kiel, then at Tübingen, where he also directed research at the Institute of Physics. In 1936 he accepted a chair at the Technical University of Berlin, where he led a nuclear fission research team and made some of the first investigations of cosmic rays. Rheumatism and the war undermined his health, and he died in the fall of 1945.

Let George Do It

The model of the ever-ready "other guy," Georges d'Amboise (1460–1510) was for over a decade the right hand of France's Louis XII. Upon Louis's accession in 1498, d'Amboise became both a cardinal of the church and first minister to the crown. In the former capacity he was disappointed in a 1503 papal bid. In the latter he was far more successful; his reforms of the courts and the tax system were effective in making his king—a blundering adventurist abroad—an extremely popular ruler at home. Louis trusted his minister so completely that it became a courtier's joke: whenever anything needed doing, it was said, the king's response would be "Let Georges do it."

Geronimo!

The paratroopers who yelled "Geronimo!" upon leaping out of their planes during World War II were, consciously or unconsciously, invoking the name of a fellow warrior whose courage they hoped they could match. Geronimo was an appropriate choice. Born Goyathlay (He Who Yawns) in 1829, the Chiricahua Apache leader was named Geronimo by settlers in northern Mexico, who apparently saw in him some of the same ascetic fire that characterized another desert dweller, St. Jerome.

The Mexicans had good reason to respect him. After his family was murdered by the Spanish in 1850, Geronimo embarked on a three-decade war against the *gringos* which led countless U.S. Army search teams on wild-goose chases throughout the Southwest. Moving on and off reservations and in and out of his mountain strongholds, he stayed ahead of both Mexican and American forces until the 1880s, when a concerted effort under Generals George Crook and Nelson Miles finally brought him to bay. Geronimo surrendered to Miles in 1886, was transported to Florida, where he remained for several years, and was settled finally in Fort Sill, Oklahoma. In his seventies, pacified at last, he sold souvenirs (of himself) at the St. Louis World's Fair and attended the inauguration of TEDDY Roosevelt. He died in 1909, in Oklahoma.

Gerrymander

In the 1960s the U.S. Supreme Court ruled that, within each state, election districts must contain approximately the same number of people. The Court said nothing, however, about districts' shape or size, thus leaving intact state legislators' traditional opportunity of redrawing the electoral map to create voter concentrations favorable to the party in power. Exercising this option is known as *gerrymandering,* from the name of the American politician who used the redistricting technique to celebrated advantage before an 1812 election.

Elbridge Gerry (1744–1814) served in the Massachusetts provincial congress and the Continental Congress before being elected in 1789 to the new nation's House of Representatives. He served there, an ardent Democratic-Republican, until 1793, and four years later served President John Adams as a negotiator over the ticklish business of French privateering. Gerry became governor of Massachusetts in 1810 and, two years later, signed a redistricting bill that blatantly concentrated his party's strength. One of the newly drawn districts wound sinuously from Gerry's hometown, Marblehead, up to Salisbury, near the New Hampshire border, suggesting to some the figure of a salamander. Federalist newspaper editor Benjamin Russell printed the new district's outline with the addition of a head, wings, and claws; the public quickly adopted his designation of the electoral beast as a *gerrymander*. Gerry became James Madison's vice president in 1812, and died halfway through his term.

Gibson Girl

The "new American woman" of the 1890s was typified by a tall, willowy creature with perfect bone structure, a huge mass of upswept, flouncy hair, and a permanent air of aristocratic calm. She was the *Gibson girl.* A kind of *Cosmopolitan* girl without the etiolated sultriness, she was created by Charles Dana Gibson (1867–1944) around 1890, and until the advent of the "flapper" in the 1920s was a premier social ideal. Not only in Gibson's own magazine drawings, but in songs and stage plays as well, she represented for millions of women a role model possessed of an agreeable balance between the energy of a new century (the Gibson girl was very athletic) and the stability of established social custom.

Born into old money in Roxbury, Massachusetts, Gibson moved as a boy to Long Island and became a talented cutter of SILHOUETTES at an early age. He studied at New York's Art Students League and later in London and Paris, sold his first drawings to humor magazines in the 1880s, and by the early 1890s was a regular story illustrator for the era's most popular literary journals, *Harper's, Scribner's,* and *Century*. His finely drawn, lightly satirical sketches of upper-middle-class life made him the eye of the "smart set" and one of the best-paid artists of his time. By 1905 he was earning an estimated $65,000 a year.

Then, at the height of his fame, Gibson gave it all up to study oil painting. For three years he toured the Mediterranean, painting and living off his savings, until he was nearly bankrupted by the panic of 1907 and had to return to his New York employers. During World War I the Gibson girl became the militant patriot, Miss Columbia. In the 1920s Gibson dabbled in entrepreneurship, managing the humor magazine *Life* into its decline. For the last decade of his life he returned to oils, concentrating on portraits and landscapes of the countryside around his Maine island summer home.

The model for many of the Gibson girl drawings was Gibson's wife, the former Irene Langhorne, whom he had married in 1895. A sister of Lady Astor (the first woman to sit in Britain's Houses of Parliament), she was the ultimate belle of America's *belle époque*.

Rube Goldberg Contraption

Although he was a man of varied talents, the American cartoonist Reuben Lucius Goldberg (1883–1970) is remembered for a single motif: the elaborate machines he designed to perform tasks that could be accomplished much more simply without them. In the typical Goldberg contraption (sometimes called simply a *Rube Goldberg*), levers, pulleys, switches, springs, and whistles interact complexly to enable someone to do something that could be done more easily without the machine—for example, mail a letter, throw a ball, or blow his nose.

Born in San Francisco on the fourth of July, Goldberg graduated from the University of California in 1904 and began his cartooning on the sports page of a San Francisco newspaper. From 1907 to 1921 he worked for the New York *Evening Mail,* where he developed such characters as Lala Palooza and Boob McNutt and gathered his drawings into the book collection *Foolish Questions* (1909). Syndicated from 1915 on, he did editorial cartoons for the New York *Sun* and *Journal American* throughout the 1940s and 1950s, and in 1948 won the PULITZER PRIZE for a cartoon about nuclear weapons. In 1963 he retired to do sculpture, and two years before his death published his lunatic designs in *Rube Goldberg vs. the Machine*.

Goldberg attributed his inventions to a fictitious professor, Lucifer Gorgonzola Butts. There is no truth to the engaging rumor that Butts was an actual person, or the head of a government agency.

Goody Two Shoes

Goody Two Shoes as a satirical epithet for a "goody-goody," or mawkishly virtuous person, comes from a children's tale that was first brought out in 1765 by John Newbery's British publishing firm and reprinted over two dozen times before the end of the century. The heroine, a poor effusive child named Goody, has only a single shoe at the outset, and when she acquires another, regales everyone who will listen with the ecstatic cry, "Two shoes!" The title of the 1775 edition suggests the tale's ponderous morality: *The History of Little Goody Two-Shoes; Otherwise called, Mrs. Margery Two-Shoes. With the Means by which she acquired her Learning and Wisdom, and in Consequence thereof her Estate. Set forth at large for the Benefit of those, Who from a state of Rags and Care, And having Shoes but half a Pair, Their Fortune and their Fame would fix, And gallop in a Coach and Six.*

Brewer supposes that this early HORATIO ALGER tale was written by Oliver Goldsmith (1730?–74). It's a conjecture, but not an unreasonable one, since the Irishman was the probable author of some of Newbery's MOTHER GOOSE rhymes and an accomplished hack-of-all-trades. Goldsmith's poem "The Deserted Village" (1770) touchingly laments the decline of country life. His *Vicar of Wake-*

field (1766) was a major contribution to the art of the eighteenth-century novel. And his most famous play, *She Stoops to Conquer* (1773), remains a staple of the comic theater.

Gordian Knot

The ancient country of Phrygia lay in what is now central Turkey. According to legend its inhabitants, promised by an oracle that their king would come to them in a wagon, seized upon a peasant named Gordius, auspiciously driving an oxcart, and immediately made him their ruler. Grateful for his good fortune, Gordius dedicated the cart to the oracle's god and tied it in place with a knot. So elaborate was his handiwork that a local tradition arose: whoever should untie the knot would rule not just Phrygia but all Asia.

The Gordian puzzle stumped all comers until Alexander the Great, already lord of the eastern Mediterranean, slashed the knot in half with his sword. Since he soon fulfilled the prophecy by subjugating everyone from Africa to India, *cutting the Gordian knot* came to mean solving an ostensibly insoluble problem. A more jaundiced view sees the young conqueror's action as hastiness rather than wit. "Alexander cut the Gordian knot," quipped writer A. T. Pierson in 1891, "which he had not the skill, patience, or strength to untie."

Gordius, if he existed, would have been king of the Phrygians around the eighth century B.C. He gave his name to the city of Gordium, now an archaeological site near Ankara, and his kingdom to his famous son, MIDAS.

Guillotine

In France under the *ancien régime,* aristocrats convicted of capital crimes were beheaded with a sword, and criminals of low birth were hanged. To Joseph Ignace Guillotin (1738–1814), this was a bad business on two counts. To have the mode of execution determined by birth was unseemly for a democratic republic; and to execute by such clumsy means as the rope and the sword was unnecessarily cruel to the condemned. A physician and a member of the revolutionary National Assembly, Guillotin therefore proposed the adoption of a uniform, and uniformly efficient, machine to dispatch enemies of the Revolution, commoners and nobles alike. The assembly approved; charged another doctor, Antoine Louis, to come up with a design; and put the first machine—called a ''Louisin'' or ''Louisette''—in operation in the spring of 1792. By the following year it had become the notoriously efficient servant of the Terror.

Two fallacies attend Guillotin's story, even today. One is that he invented the device himself, when in fact a guillotine-type beheading instrument had been used in Europe since the Middle Ages, under the curious nickname ''the Maiden.'' The other is that he was himself guillotined, as a kind of poetic injustice. Antoine Louis was guillotined (or ''louisined''), but not his more famous colleague. Imprisoned during the Terror, Guillotin was indeed condemned; but he escaped the blade after Robespierre's fall and went on to play a major role in the establishment of the French Academy of Medicine. He hated the popular designation *guillotine,* and argued against it his whole life. After his death his children petitioned the government to have the device renamed; as Robert Hendrickson points out, all the government would grant them was the right to have their own name changed.

Guy

This common American equivalent for the British ''fellow'' or ''chap'' derives, by a somewhat circuitous route, from the name of an English malcontent famous for his failure to blow up Parliament. Born in 1570, Guy Fawkes was a Roman Catholic convert who bitterly resented the anti-Romanist reforms of James I. With a group of conspirators, he planted barrels of black powder underneath the Houses of Parliament in the fall of 1605, intending to ignite them on November 5, when the king opened the assembly. The so-called Gunpowder Plot was betrayed; Fawkes was arrested, tortured into a confession, and executed in January of the following year. But he was not forgotten. November 5 continues to be celebrated in England as Guy Fawkes Day—a rare instance of a celebration commemorating an event that did *not* happen.

It became traditional on Guy Fawkes Day to burn effigies of "the old Guy," and because effigies seldom sport the latest fashions, "guy" became by the early nineteenth century a synonym for "tatterdemalion" or "ragamuffin." Americans extended the connotation so that, by the 1890s in the States, *guy* meant any male, regardless of dress.

Paul Beale, the assiduous editor of Partridge's eighth edition, suggests a linkage with Yiddish *goy,* for "Gentile." Since both *guy* and a vast wave of Jewish immigrants entered the New World about the same time, it's a fruitful, if facetious, suggestion.

Guns

The discovery of gunpowder by the Chinese has proved to be an enormous boon to human invention. In the nineteenth century particularly—that heyday of the small-arms aficionado—not a decade passed in which some savvy ballistophile did not find new uses for saltpeter, charcoal, and flying metal. Herewith a few milestones:

Shrapnel

The modern hand grenade, designed to disperse lethal metal fragments, or *shrapnel,* over a wide area, derives from a spherical model developed around 1800 by a British ordnance officer. Henry Shrapnel (1761–1842) was commissioned in the Royal Artillery in 1779, served overseas for two decades, and produced his *shrapnel shot* just in time for George III's troops to use it in their 1804 invasion of Dutch Surinam.

Colt Revolver

Variously known as the six-shooter, the Peacemaker, and the gun that won the West, Samuel Colt's famous revolver was the most widely sold handgun in nineteenth-century America. The son of a Yankee textile manufacturer, Colt (1814–62) also invented a remote-control naval mine and an underwater telegraph cable. The cocking device which he patented for his original (1836) revolver remains the model for revolver mechanisms today.

Derringer

Designed and produced by Philadelphia gunsmith Henry Deringer, Jr., the *derringer* was a palm-sized pistol that was extremely popular in the 1840s and 1850s in the United States. A lady's handbag gun and gambler's sidearm, the derringer served as the ideal concealed weapon: it was the gun that John Wilkes Booth had in his pocket in Ford's Theater on the night of April 14, 1865.

Minnie Ball

To add speed and accuracy to the shot, the bores of firearms were spirally grooved, or "rifled," as early as the fifteenth century. The effectiveness of the procedure, however, was hampered by an inability to produce shot small enough to be muzzle-loaded yet large enough to grip the rifling when fired. French inventor Claude Etienne Minié solved this problem in the mid-nineteenth century with a ball that was slightly swelled by gas pressure upon firing. The *minnie ball* greatly improved the slaughter statistics in the American Civil War.

Sharps Buffalo Gun

The hordes of buffalo that roamed the American prairies in the early nineteenth century cried out for a hunting weapon that could be manipulated more quickly on horseback than the muzzle-loaded flintlock. Christian Sharps (1811–74) answered the call in 1850 with a breech-loading gun, and by 1854 was mass-producing it in a Hartford, Connecticut, factory. So telling was its accuracy that the inventor's name survives in the term *sharpshooter*.

Winchester 73

The lever-action *Winchester 73* is the gun that Woody Strode throws to John Wayne in *The Man Who Shot Liberty Valance*. It is the gun that rides with the Marlboro Man and that the Daisy Air Rifle is modeled on. Its manufacturer, Oliver Fisher Winchester (1810–60), founded the Winchester Repeating Arms Company, contributed heavily to philanthropies, and in 1866 was elected lieutenant governor of Connecticut.

Gatling Gun

Richard Gatling (1818–1903) was a case study in turning plowshares into swords. Having made a fortune inventing farming equipment, he gave the Civil War its most modern and devastating weapon, a crank-operated, rotary-firing machine gun that was U.S. Army issue from 1866 until 1911, when the automatic-firing MAXIM gun made it obsolete. The gangster slang term *gat,* for a handgun, also comes from Gatling's name.

Maxim Gun

The belt-fed, water-cooled machine gun developed by Hiram S. Maxim (1840–1916) in 1884 remained the state of the art in rapid fire from the turn of the century until World War II. The highly specialized Maxim clan also included Hiram's brother Hudson, who developed smokeless powder and artillery shells for World War I, and his son Hiram P., inventor of the rifle silencer.

M1 and M16 Rifles

Contemporary bolt-action rifles are based on a model first produced successfully in 1867 by German inventor Paul Mauser. Mauser ("M") type rifles have been the infantryman's companion through two world wars and countless other conflicts. The Springfield M1 was standard U.S. issue until 1936, when the M1 *Garand* (after inventor John C. Garand) replaced it. The Garand was itself superseded by the automatic M16.

Tommy Gun

The lightweight submachine gun favored by the first Irish Republican Army and "violin"-toting bootleggers was invented in 1920 by U.S. Army officer John T. Thompson (1860–1940), head of the service's Small Arms Division in World War I. Often depicted as a criminal's special, the Thompson, or *tommy*, gun was also widely used by the American military, beginning with the U.S. invasion of Nicaragua in 1925.

H–J

Halley's Comet

This most famous of comets, which even as I write is faintly visible out near the sword of Orion, has been observed from the Earth twenty times since 239 B.C. Not until 1705, however, did scientists understand that all these sightings were of the same celestial body. In that year the English astronomer Edmund Halley (1656–1742) published a paper on cometary orbits, predicting that the comet he had observed in 1682 would reappear in 1758. When it did, not only were the Newtonian mechanics on which Halley based his findings thoroughly vindicated, but the comet was named in his honor.

The discovery of the comet's seventy-six-year period was only one of Halley's accomplishments. Graduated from Oxford in 1676, he made his reputation by issuing a standard star catalogue of the southern hemisphere, and was made a member of the Royal Society at twenty-two. Settled in London in 1682, he worked out a method for determining longitude at sea, served as deputy comptroller of the Chester mint, and was directly responsible for convincing a reluctant Isaac Newton to publish his masterpiece, *Principia Mathematica* (1687). Professor of geometry at Oxford from 1704 until his death, Halley translated the works of classical mathematicians and, in 1718, after comparing his own star positions with those of Ptolemy, became the first person publicly to deny the "fixed star" theory of the ancients. The crown recognized his many achievements in 1720 by appointing him astronomer royal.

John Hancock

Signing the Declaration of Independence first was no more than John Hancock's right, since in the summer of 1776 he was president of the Continental Congress. But Hancock was one of the colonies' most avid publicity hounds, and being first wasn't enough. Explaining that he wanted King George to be able to read his name without spectacles, he signed with an outsized flourish that ever since has made *John Hancock* a colloquialism for "signature."

Born in 1737 in what is now Quincy, Massachusetts, Hancock was adopted as a child by his paternal uncle Thomas, the wealthiest merchant in Boston. He inherited Thomas's fortune in 1764, and it seems likely he opposed British revenue measures as much out of personal financial concerns as out of patriotic zeal. Samuel Adams, perceiving the value of having a rich merchant on the American side, guided Hancock's political career, which included service in 1774 as president of the Massachusetts congress and as delegate one year later to the Continental Congress. Twice elected that body's president, he resigned in 1777, miffed that his colleagues had preferred Washington to him as head of the continental army.

Hancock's vanity and ambition did not make him one of the nobler Founding Fathers, but his material and vocal support of the cause, in the *Dictionary of American Biography*'s coy summation, "made him immensely popular with those who did not work with him so closely as to perceive that his mind was of mediocre quality." Among these myopic enthusiasts were the citizens of Hancock's home state, who elected him governor nine times. He served first in 1780, and was regularly returned until 1785. At that point, with rural uprisings brewing, Hancock conveniently resigned, leaving his successor, James Bowdoin, to deal with Shays' Rebellion. Once the disturbances were quelled, Hancock was elected again, and he was still in office upon his death in 1793.

Sadie Hawkins Day

Sadie Hawkins Day is a nonofficial American holiday on which any unattached male is forced to marry the woman who catches him. This curious bit of cryptomisogynistic fakelore was invented by cartoonist Al Capp in his extremely popular strip *L'il Abner*. Capp made full use of the opportunities in the idea for insulting the conventionally unattractive, and the holiday has always appealed most to the puerile—specifically, to high school and college students, who in the 1940s and 1950s frequently staged mock marriages and dances on the first Saturday in November in honor of the supposedly man-hungry Miss Hawkins.

Capp's given name was Alfred Gerald Caplin. Born in 1909, he studied at the Museum School of Fine Arts in Boston and did work on Ham Fisher's Joe PALOOKA comic strip before introducing *L'il Abner* in 1934. By the end of World War II the activities of Dogpatch residents L'il Abner, Daisy Mae, and the Yokums were being followed week after week by approximately 25 million readers. Often politically controversial, the strip ran until 1977, a year before its creator's death.

Heimlich Maneuver

Although choking on food remains a major cause of death among children, the incidence of this tragedy has been dramatically reduced in the past decade by the introduction of the Heimlich maneuver. A method of purging obstructions from the esophagus by the application of sharp pressure on the abdomen, it was developed by Henry Jay Heimlich (1920–), a physician and surgeon long interested in disorders of the alimentary tract. Educated at Cornell medical school, Heimlich did his initial work in New York City, then transferred to Cincinnati, where since 1977 he has been professor of advanced clinical sciences at Xavier University. His publications include books on thoracic and stomach surgery. The procedure by which he is known is demonstrated in his 1976 film *How to Save a Choking Victim: The Heimlich Maneuver*. He is also the originator of the so-called *Heimlich operation*, for the replacement of the esophagus, and of a surgical chest drain valve. In the 1980 *Who's Who in America,* he identifies his current concerns as reaching beyond the operating room: "My ultimate goal," he writes, "is to avoid needless death and promote well-being for the largest number of people by establishing a philosophy that will eliminate war."

Herculean Task

A seemingly impossible task is sometimes called *herculean* after the mythical hero most popular with the makers of tunic-and-sandal epics: Hercules. He is the bastard son of Zeus by the mortal woman Alcmene and, like the other products of Zeus's lust, inevitably incurs Hera's wrath. She first tries to kill him in his cradle but is foiled when the infant strangles the serpents she has sent to do him in. Years later, when he is grown, she makes him mad, so that he kills six of his children. When Hercules asks the oracle at Delphi to offer him a means of atonement, the oracle sends him to Argos, where the Argive king Eurystheus tells him to perform twelve labors. They include such bagatelles as killing the nine-headed Hydra; cleaning the AUGEAN STABLES; stealing the girdle of Hippolyta, queen of the AMAZONS; capturing Cerberus, the three-headed guard dog of Hades; and stealing the golden apples of the Hesperides. These twelve labors—all of which Hercules accomplishes—are the model for our "herculean" tasks.

Hippocratic Oath

The Greek physician Hippocrates was born on the island of Cos around 460 B.C. and died, somewhere in the Mediterranean, eighty or ninety years later. That is all we know of his life, and yet he has become known as the father of all Western medicine because of two remarkable legacies. The first is the series of treatises that scholars call the Hippocratic Collection, in which Hippocrates and/or his followers laid the foundations for a naturalistic understanding of disease; that their interpretations of natural causes were erroneous is less important than the fact that, in refuting the traditional ancient view that the gods were behind all human ills, the Hippocratic school paved the way for scientific thought. The second legacy is the document widely known as the *Hippocratic oath*.

The oath, which laid down the physician's obligations to his colleagues and his patients, is still administered in modified form to the graduates of many medical schools and still invoked by medical partisans who believe it enshrines, or exposes, common practice. Defenders of the medical status quo call the oath's basic precept—that the doctor should help, not harm, the patient—a fair description of how physicians operate. Critics of establishment practices call it the Hypocritic Oath.

In 1948 the World Medical Association, meeting in Geneva, drew up a form of the oath that excised supposedly outdated provisions: the ideas, for example, that physicians should maintain trade secrets, that they should reimburse needy teachers for their instruction, and that they should refrain from encouraging abortions. Continually debated and "adjusted," the oath remains nevertheless a capsule definition, at least in theory, of what medical ethics ought to be.

Hobson's Choice

When you ask to see a pair of shoes and are told you can have them in any color "as long as it's black," you are being given *Hobson's choice*. The term means "no choice at all"; someone who offers it to you really means "Take it or leave it." The phrase arose in Elizabethan England to describe a peculiar business policy of one Thomas Hobson (1544–1630), who rented horses for travel between the cities of Cambridge and London. In order to ensure that his animals were given approximately equal amounts of wear and tear, he let them out only on a rotating basis. Customers were allowed to view his entire riding stock, but could take no horse out of its turn. Their alternatives were the animal nearest the stable door—or nothing.

To judge by his business success, Hobson was anything but the niggling, unimaginative manager that his horse-leasing policy might suggest. He amassed a huge fortune in his lifetime, owned half a dozen manor houses, and at his death provided for the perpetual maintenance of a public aqueduct and fountain in the Cambridge marketplace. The poet John Milton thought enough of him to devote two humorous epitaphs to him at his death.

Hooligan

The original of *hooligan,* for "ruffian," was almost certainly an Irish tough (or toughs) living in London in the mid- to late nineteenth century. The sources differ on identity, but I agree with Robert Hendrickson and Paul Beale that the nod should probably go to one particularly notorious troublemaker, Patrick Hooligan, who made the lives of Southwark residents unenviable just before the turn of the century. According to Clarence Rook's memoir, *The Hooligan Nights* (1899), Patrick frequented the Lamb and Flag pub in Irish Court and was chiefly interested, as he "walked to and fro among his fellow men," in "robbing them and occasionally bashing them." He was, Rook says, as real as Buddha or Mohammed, and his exploits just as prone to embroidery, so that when he died (in a hospital jail) he left behind him "a great tradition . . . a cult." The cult, like that of the THUGS, may have died; but the tradition is, alas, alive and well.

According to Hoyle

The expression *according to Hoyle* has somewhat the same force in English as the Yiddish dietary epithet "kosher": both suggest conformity to established rules. The former phrase evokes Edmond Hoyle (1672–1769), who spent the bulk of his long life as an obscure barrister and at the age of seventy made a name for himself as an authority on parlor games. His *Short Treatise on the Game of Whist* (1742) was a fast success, was reprinted over a dozen times in his lifetime, and remained the bible for London's whist clubs—the forerunners of today's bridge circles—for over a hundred years. Subsequent treatises on backgammon

(1743) and chess (1761) were also well received, helping to make Hoyle's name a synonym for "the last word." Modern compendia of game regulations continue to trade on the name, although contemporary "Hoyles" contain the rules for many games that did not exist in his day.

Jacobin

The "Jacobin" tag for those holding radical political opinions dates from the French Revolution. The term had long been applied to members of the Dominican religious order because their original Paris house was situated in the rue St. Jacques. It was in a former Dominican, or *Jacobin,* convent that the most extreme revolutionary party held its first meetings in 1789, and the epithet was quickly secularized. Thus, in a bizarre affirmation of the adage that politics makes strange bedfellows, the name of gentle St. James (Jacques in French, Jacobus in Latin) came to be attached to those of Danton and Marat and Robespierre.

Jacobin must be distinguished from various near homonym cousins. *Jacobean* refers to the age of England's James I (1603–25), which produced English Renaissance architecture; the mature work of Shakespeare, Jonson, and Donne; and the King James version of the Bible. *Jacobian* refers to the work of the German mathematician Karl G. J. Jacobi (1804–51), a major contributor to the theory of functions. And *Jacobite* applies to the followers of England's last Stuart king, James II, who after his exile in 1688 waged a half century of fruitless war for the return of the Stuart line.

Jekyll/Hyde Personality

The erratic behavior that popular psychologists today ascribe to "mood swing" was first definitively portrayed not in a professional journal but in Robert Louis Stevenson's 1886 novel *Dr. Jekyll and Mr. Hyde,* in which the eminently reasonable physician Henry Jekyll is destroyed by his own dark half, Mr. Hyde. In this extremely popular work, the Scottish writer probed ancient questions regarding the nature of evil and foreshadowed FREUDIAN psychology, in which the human ego is torn between a stiffly proper superego and a violent, devouring id.

One of the most accomplished popular writers of the nineteenth century, Stevenson (1850–94) lived a frenetic, globe-trotting existence in spite of chronic tuberculosis. Beginning his literary career as a travel writer, he achieved fame with the novel *Treasure Island* (1883), and followed it with the classic romances *Kidnapped* (1886) and *The Master of Ballantrae* (1888). Children know him best as the author of *A Child's Garden of Verses* (1885), and horror fans worldwide have applauded the subtleties of the Jekyll/Hyde tale.

Stevenson and his wife spent his last years on an island retreat in Samoa, where he dictated his unfinished masterpiece *Weir of Hermiston*. The work he left behind, in addition to absorbing generations of readers, has also proved a rich vein for Hollywood. The 1938 *Kidnapped* was a showcase for child actor Freddie Bartholomew, as was the 1950 *Treasure Island* for that memorable Long John Silver, Robert Newton. The Jekyll/Hyde character, an inventive actor's delight, was done without makeup in 1920 by John Barrymore, won Fredric March a 1932 OSCAR, and was redone nine years later by Spencer Tracy.

Jeremiad

WEBSTER defines *jeremiad* as "a prolonged lamentation or complaint." The original such lamentation was the Old Testament book Lamentations, traditionally ascribed to the prophet Jeremiah, who lived in the sixth century B.C. and who may have witnessed the destruction of Jerusalem in 586 B.C. by the Babylonian king Nebuchadnezzar. The style of Lamentations is both monitory and optimistic: identifying the decline of Jewish power as a result of moral corruption, the author also prefigures the New Testament "new covenant" based on repentance and final redemption. Whether or not the prophet was in fact the writer of the book (authorities do not agree), a sense of woeful, apocalyptic dread is indelibly associated with his name. Invoking Webster once again, we find that *Jeremiah* used as a noun means "one who is pessimistic about the present and foresees a calamitous future."

Jezebel

Since the sixteenth century at least, the term *jezebel* has been loosely applied to any woman of high spirits and low morals. The connotation survives even in our modern, more "liberal" century. Witness, for example, the role of the flamboyant, slightly tartish southern belle which won Bette Davis her second OSCAR in the 1938 film *Jezebel*. Or today's Biblical fundamentalists, for whom the original Jezebel is the archetypal "wicked woman," the forerunner of all the modern hussies who prefer rock music and lipstick to the Word.

The original Jezebel was a Tyrian princess who, after marrying the Jewish king Ahab, set about supplanting the worship of Jehovah with that of the Phoenician god Baal. She is not an attractive character—she arranges the wholesale slaughter of the Lord's prophets—but the story of her wickedness (told in Kings) does not make it terribly clear why she came to represent female wantonness. The passage where she lasciviously paints her face (II Kings 9:30) is hardly a sign of seductiveness, but rather a ritual preparation for her death at the hands of the avenging Jehu, a politically ambitious follower of the Lord who at the urging of Elijah overthrows the Ahab dynasty, slaughters all devotees of Baal, and makes himself king of Israel.

The Jehu-Elijah combination proved a fierce one for the painted woman. Jehu has her thrown from a window, tramples her with his horse, then goes in to eat dinner while, fulfilling Elijah's prophecy, her body is devoured by dogs. He also manages, in recompense for Jezebel's savagery to Israel's holy men, to eliminate the prophets of Baal. Contemporary Bible-thumbers may take solace in Jehu's brand of harsh justice, but more charitable minds have demurred. In the 1910 *Temple Dictionary of the Bible*, for example, we read this sympathetic gloss on her end: "It was a queenly figure that greeted Jehu the regicide with such disdain. It is impossible to justify that coarse plebian in his brutal treatment of the aged princess of Tyre.''

Jonah

A *Jonah* is a jinx. That's what WEBSTER says, and it was also the opinion of the sailors who put out to sea with the prophet in the Old Testament Book of Jonah. En route from Joppa to Tarshish, they were beset by a terrible storm, and when they cast lots to discover the cause, it turned out that Jonah was the culprit. He had refused the Lord's command to ''cry against'' the wickedness of Nineveh, and this was his (and their) punishment. So they threw him overboard, at his own request. He was swallowed by a ''great fish'' and after three days was vomited out on dry land. No dummy, he headed right for Nineveh.

Jonah proved to be a better preacher than a crewman. With the shortest prophecy on record—''Yet forty days and Nineveh shall be overthrown''—he converted the entire city to fasting, and the Lord, being merciful, let them off. This was not what Jonah had in mind. Bitter at the failure of his promise, he went out to sit in the sun—whereupon God proceeded to teach him a second lesson in humility. He grew a gourd plant for Jonah as a parasol, and then, just as the prophet was getting used to the shade, withered it down to a reed. Taunting Jonah about the one-day cabana, He said, in effect, You didn't cut down the gourd plant, so I won't cut down the city. It's a little difficult to imagine why God would want to save Nineveh as much as Jonah would want to save the plant. But that's parables for you.

Whatever the reason, the Book of Jonah ends with a description of lucky Nineveh that is both touching and droll. Why should I not spare ''that great city,'' the Lord asks rhetorically, ''wherein are more than sixscore thousand persons that cannot discern between their right hand and their left hand; and also much cattle?'' I take that last phrase about the cattle as proof not necessarily that God exists, but surely that He created Woody Allen.

A variation of Jonah could be *Davy Jones*. In sailor's slang Davy Jones is a traditional evil spirit of the sea, and to *go to Davy*

Jones's locker is to be drowned or buried at sea—that is, to go to the bottom. Because of the connotations of ill luck here, *Jones* is often considered a corruption of *Jonah. Davy* is variously interpreted as a form of the West Indian *duffy,* for "ghost"; or a diminutive of the Welsh *St. David,* to whom sailors often prayed for protection.

Keeping Up with the Joneses

The original Joneses were the creation of cartoonist Arthur R. Momand, whose comic strip *Keeping Up with the Joneses* ran successfully in American newspapers from 1913 to 1931, when it failed to keep up with the Depression. Robert Hendrickson reports that "Pop" Momand selected his title in recollection of the hard times he and his wife had experienced in New York's posh Cedarhurst community just after the turn of the century. An earlier working title had been *Keeping Up with the Smiths*. Momand rejected that on the grounds of euphony—the same grounds that had caused Tennyson, blessedly, to bury this prototype of the most famous line in his *Tithonus:* "After many a summer dies the duck."

Josh

Although the derivation of this American slang term from the pen name of the humorist Josh Billings (1818–85) is not strictly provable, both appropriateness and chronology argue in its behalf. The term was first used as a synonym for "banter" or "joke" shortly after Billings's death, and *joshing* was certainly a fit description for the peculiar brand of rustic comedy that he popularized in hundreds of essays.

Billings's real name was Henry Wheeler Shaw. Like Mark Twain, he learned the basics of his comic craft from the example of Artemus Ward and, like Twain, he enjoyed considerable acclaim after the Civil War as a lecturing pundit. Unlike Twain, however, he was nearly fifty when he turned to writing, having spent decades in various occupations, notably real estate and auctioneering. The flavor of his wit is suggested by a selection from his first success, the 1864 "Essa on the Muel":

> Tha are the strongest creeturs on earth, and heaviest ackording tu their sise; I herd tell ov one who fell oph from the tow path, on the Eri kanawl, and sunk as soon as he touched bottom, but he kept rite on towing the boat tu the nex stashun, breathing thru his ears, which stuck out of the water about 2 feet 6 inches; i did'nt see this did, but an auctioneer told me of it, and i never knew an auctioneer tu lie unless it was absolutely convenient.

Shaw/Billings frequently enlisted animals as foils for his wit, as in his essay on "How Tew Pik Out a Dog," where he recommends a wooden dog over a real one, since wooden dogs do not stray or catch rabies; or in his description of salted cod as "good eating for a wet day; they are better than an umbreller to keep a man dry." He also excelled at the aphoristic dig: "Most people," he wrote in a collection of "Shooting Stars," are "like an egg, too phull oy themselfs to hold enny thing else."

Billings's witticisms were collected in the 1865 volume *Sayings,* in a series of jocular *Allminax* (1868–79) that parodied the famous *Farmer's Almanacs,* and posthumously in a four-volume collected works. One of the most famous "cracker-barrel philosophers" of his time, he has been called "AESOP and Ben Franklin, condensed and abridged."

Jovial

Jovial, and the expression *by Jove,* come from the proper name *Jove,* a classical variant of *Jupiter*. Jupiter, the Roman equivalent of the Greeks' Zeus, was the supreme ruler of the gods, and the father of many: his name may derive from *deus pater* (father-god) or *dies pater* (father-day). Since neither Jupiter nor Zeus was known as a particularly mirthful deity, the modern meaning of *jovial* seems a puzzle. The solution lies in Renaissance astrology, whose practitioners were convinced that the *planet* Jupiter extended a favorable, indeed blissful, natal influence. Thus *jovial,* which hearkens back to stern Zeus, came to mean "cheery and bright."

Don Juan

Don Juan as an epithet for a successful but unscrupulous ladies' man derives from the name of the hero in a seventeenth-century Spanish play. *El Burlador de Sevilla y el Conviadado de Piedra* (The Libertine of Seville and the Stone Guest) was written in 1630 by the extremely prolific dramatist Tirso de Molina (ca. 1583–1648). It established all the conventions of the Don Juan legend as we know it: a dissolute Spanish nobleman, Don Juan Tenorio, kills the father of one of his conquests in a duel, dines with a statue of the murdered man, and is cast into Hell for his sins. The play is dated, but Tirso's central character, torn between profligacy and piety, has fascinated the Western mind for three centuries. He makes memorable reappearances in, among other works, Byron's satirical epic *Don Juan,* Mozart's opera *Don Giovanni,* and Shaw's rollicking philosophical interlude, the "Don Juan in Hell" sequence of his play *Man and Superman.*

Tirso de Molina was the pen name of the friar Gabriel Téllez, a younger contemporary of Cervantes who wrote about 300 plays in spite of official church resistance. Next to *El Burlador,* his best-known drama is a sophisticated study of free will, *El Condenado por Desconfiado* (Condemned for Despair), published in 1635. He also wrote poetry and stories.

Juggernaut

Juggernaut is a variant of *Jagganath,* a cult title of the supreme Hindu god Vishnu. The use of the name to mean an irresistible, generally destructive force arose among European visitors to India who witnessed, as early as the fourteenth century, the dramatic procession at Puri in which a huge statue of the god is wheeled on a cart from one of his sanctuaries to another. Occasionally, overzealous or simply careless bystanders were crushed beneath the wheels of the vehicle, and Western viewers, taking these accidents as intentional, portrayed Jagganath as an instrument of blind mayhem; hence the modern connotation. It is a connotation that would surprise any Hindu, since Vishnu is a kindly deity, the protector and preserver of the world; the idea that a worshiper would sacrifice himself at the Puri festival a Hindu would see as either sacrilegious or absurd.

John and Jack

Since the Middle Ages, *John* has been one of the most popular, if not the most popular, of English names. As E. C. Brewer pointed out over a hundred years ago, this is probably due to the fact that it is the name of several well-known Christian saints, including most notably St. John the Evangelist and St. John the Baptist. Because the name has always been common, it has given rise to a host of catch phrases and other idioms that look like bona-fide eponyms but that cannot be traced to real persons. In this category appear such expressions as *johnny-come-lately,* for an intruder; *johnny-on-the-spot,* for a fortuitous arrival; the medieval fiction *John Doe;* the somewhat later slang term *John Barleycorn,* for the beverage made from barley, that is, whiskey; and the hooker's term *john,* for a client, which illustrates better than most terms the facelessness of the expression. The Americanisms *Johnny Reb* (for a Confederate soldier) and *John Q. Public* (for a common citizen) are also examples of this usage.

Two usages are arguably less generic. *John Bull* as the representative Englishman comes from the satirist John Arbuthnot's 1712 work *Law Is a Bottomless Pit,* in which Bull is an outspoken, earnest farmer. And *john* as a synonym for "toilet" has been associated with the worthy Sir John Harrington, who was reputed to have invented a primitive flush toilet during the reign of Elizabeth I.

The same fusion into impersonality occurs with *Jack*. Early on in English popular speech Jack was a term for any male, especially a young or hearty one. Hence the dubiously eponymous *Jack Frost; Jack Sprat, Jack Horner,* and *Jack and Jill* of the nursery rhymes; and *jacks, jackpot, jack-in-the-box,* and *jackstraw* of the games (this last term may refer to Jack Straw, a leader in the 1381 English peasants' rebellion).

From this original diffuse meaning arose a profusion of slang terms, most of them divisible into two basic classes. One class includes those terms that refer specifically to the male of the species: *jackrabbit, jackass, jackdaw,* and the sturdily redundant *man jack*. The other includes those terms that, as the *Oxford English Dictionary* puts it, refer to "things which in some way take the place of a lad or man, or save human labor." Hence *jackhammer, jackboot, jackknife, jacklight,* and the mechanic's old reliable, plain *jack*.

Jack-o'-lantern is a special case. It derives from an old Irish tale in which the protagonist, a notorious drinker named Jack, twice tricks the Devil out of his soul and is eventually punished by being made to wander the earth forever, like Cain. The Devil hurls a flaming coal at him as a parting gesture, and this Jack places inside a hollowed-out turnip, thus creating the first jack-o'-lantern.

Crackerjack and *flapjack* are fanciful constructions that are not very likely eponymous. In nineteenth-century England, *crackerjack* was a sailor's term for crackers mixed with salted meat. At the same time in the United States *flapjack* was a slang term for "somersault."

K–L

Kilroy Was Here

Throughout World War II and for many years afterward, this cryptic signature was probably the most widely observed piece of graffiti in the world. Often accompanied by a crude drawing of a face peering over a wall, it appeared first in military installations and soon spread to public and privy walls from Houston to Hong Kong. Kilroy, whoever he was, showed an ingenious facility for signing in at inaccessible places, such as the hulls of battleships and the torch of the Statue of Liberty. By war's end coverage of the Kilroy phenomenon in the popular press had generated widespread, and often bizarre, speculation about the original writer's identity and motivation. Theories ranged from the mundane (the first Kilroy was an infantryman bearding the Air Force for its claim that it arrived everywhere first) to the psychoanalytical (the craze was a collective Oedipal fantasy celebrating the death of the *roi,* or king—see OEDIPUS COMPLEX).

Numerous contenders stepped forward to claim the title of "original" Kilroy. The most plausible claim—and the one generally accepted today—was put forth by a Quincy, Massachusetts, shipyard worker named James J. Kilroy, who said that he had first painted the famous line on the hull of the carrier *Lexington* as a notice to his supervisors that he was performing his job. This inspector's tag was then copied by scribblers around the world. Kilroy himself, although he stopped signing his work after the war, continued to work at the shipyard until his death in 1962.

Kinsey Reports

If sexual activity is any less taboo a subject now than it was in the first half of the century, the change ultimately is due less to Masters and Johnson's *Human Sexual Response* or to *Playboy* magazine than to a pair of dry and bulky treatises by the American researcher Alfred Charles Kinsey (1894–1956). The notorious *Kinsey reports* anticipated the entire so-called sexual revolution and set the immediate stage, in the early 1950s, for Hugh Hefner's reprurientation of our mores.

Born in Hoboken, New Jersey, Kinsey took a zoology doctorate at Harvard and in 1920 joined the faculty of Indiana University. For the next two decades he applied himself to entomology, becoming the world's acknowledged expert on the gall wasp. In 1942, his interest shifting to an ostensibly more complex species, he established the university's Institute for Sex Research, and six years later, with two Indiana colleagues, published the first of the institute's reports, *Sexual Behavior in the Human Male*. It was followed in 1953—the year of *Playboy*'s debut—by a companion volume on female sexuality. Both volumes were instant best-sellers, and although Kinsey did not live to witness the social ramifications of his labors, he was able to ensure the survival of his institute with royalties from the books' sales.

In an era when sexologists have become as numerous as gall wasps, it is easy to overlook Kinsey's contribution. We are accustomed to the point of ennui to hearing about mean frequencies of marital intercourse, the physiology of orgasm, and kaleidoscopes of erotic inclination. Before 1948 such subjects were discussed only behind ivied walls or in smut shops. Kinsey brought them out of these cloisters, with a rattling social effect. His first report vied for top honors on the best-seller list with Eisenhower's European memoirs and self-help books by established authors Dale Carnegie and Joshua Liebman. The "female" volume pushed everything else aside except Norman Vincent Peale's *Power of Positive Thinking* and the new Revised Standard Version of the Bible. And it was still thirteen years before Masters and Johnson.

Klieg Light

The carbon arc lamps which have been used in the lighting of motion picture sets since the silent era were originally called "Kliegl lights" after their inventors. They were the brothers John H. Kliegl (1869–1959) and Anton T. Kliegl (1872–1927), who emigrated from their native Germany to America just as the film industry was getting started and in 1897 established a family firm, Kliegl Brothers, to produce and market lighting equipment. The final "l" was dropped early on, and the brothers' design became standard in stage as well as screen production.

Levi's

The original Levi's manufacturer was the redoubtable Levi Strauss (1829–1902), a Bavarian immigrant who landed in New York as a teenager with not a Mark in his pocket. His start in the New World was selling dry goods and household notions for his brothers, who had emigrated earlier and who shipped goods as far south as Kentucky. He might have stayed in the East but for an 1849 phenomenon: the California Gold Rush. In 1853, the twenty-four-year-old Strauss took a clipper ship to San Francisco, intending to sell to the miners.

He came west loaded with canvas, expecting to sell it for tents. He soon discovered that in the rough-and-tumble world of the diggings there was a greater need for PANTS that wore well. Young Strauss set about to fill that need. He arranged for the canvas to be tailored and began selling the original *Levi's* (as the miners called them) from a small shop on Sacramento Street. By the late 1860s he had switched the fabric to denim, introduced an indigo dye—and invented the American blue jean. ("Jean" is from *geane fustian,* a cloth that originated in sixteenth-century Genoa.) Strauss gave his wares a personal stamp in 1873 when, in a joint venture with a Nevada tailor named Jacob Davis, he patented the copper riveting of stress points, still a distinctive Levi Strauss trademark.

With that patent the modern Levi Strauss company was born. It grew slowly (Levi's were not introduced east of the Mississippi until the 1930s) but under extremely sure hands. The innovative thinking that the founder had brought to the company continued in his successors, in both the social and the financial spheres. In 1906, after the San Francisco earthquake destroyed the Strauss factory, management kept workers on at full pay. In 1915 the company introduced the garment industry's first assembly line. Today, boasting $2 billion in sales each year, Strauss's brainchild is the largest clothing dealer in the world—and a prototype of the socially responsible corporation.

Strauss himself lived out his life in San Francisco, a bachelor with strong family sentiments (the company today is controlled by descendents of Levi's nephews) and a businessman committed to social service (he endowed over two dozen scholarships at the University of California). His most famous creation, the Levi's jean, is part of the permanent collection of the Smithsonian Institution; the Strauss company, in its brochure "Everybody Knows His First Name," does not exaggerate when it calls itself "an American tradition, symbolizing the vitality of the West to people all over the world."

Lucullan Feast

The adjective *Lucullan,* invariably followed by "feast" or "banquet," suggests the exacting tastes of a gourmet coupled with extravagant splendor. The first so-named affairs were hosted by Lucius Licinius Lucullus (ca. 117–56 B.C.), a Roman general and statesman whose political and military accomplishments have been overshadowed by his gustatory zeal. A protégé of the dictator Sulla, he led armies against Mithradates in Asia, governed the province of Africa, and in 74 B.C. served as Rome's chief executive, or consul.

Upon his recall to Rome from a second war against Mithradates in 66 B.C., Lucullus, having amassed a sizable fortune, devoted himself to sumptuous living. His dining rooms were said to be coded, so that his chef, knowing only the room, would understand exactly what level of display his master demanded that evening. He is said to have introduced cherries into Italy and, according to

Horace, to have owned 5,000 purple robes. He was also a patron of the arts, although that fact, like his military record, has long since been drowned in stories of wine and song.

Luddite

Workers who destroy their employers' working capital, especially machinery, are known as *Luddites* after the brief and ill-fated Luddite movement in early nineteenth-century England. Toward the end of 1811, frustrated in their attempts to secure passage of a minimum wage bill, hosiery workers in the Midlands began to smash the weaving frames that employers, under the prevailing cottage industry system, had stationed in their homes. Blame for this industrial vandalism was typically laid at the door of "King Ludd" or "Ned Ludd"—a catchall cover that was designed to protect the workers actually responsible, and that gave a name to the movement.

Although most sources agree that Ludd was a mythical leader, there is some anecdotal evidence that he may have had a historical model. The eleventh edition of the *Encyclopaedia Britannica* (1911) cites an 1847 biography of one Lord Sidmouth which says that Ned Ludd was a feebleminded and much abused Leicestershire lad who, being unable to catch his tormentors one particularly vexing day, smashed some stocking frames in frustration; "afterwards, whenever any frames were broken, it became a common saying that Ludd had done it."

The Luddite movement, a violent prefiguring of the resentment now being felt about automation, succeeded in improving work conditions briefly, but it was brutally put down in 1813, with the hanging of several of its leaders. It thus stands as an abortive but significant prelude to the more solid reform work of midcentury.

Lynch Law

In the year 1780 the God-fearing folk of Virginia's Pittsylvania County, down on the Carolina border, were being preyed on by gangs of young toughs whom the appointed authorities could not apprehend. To put an end to their pillaging and brigandage, a group of citizens led by militia captain William Lynch (1742–1820) formed a vigilante ''association'' whose official compact pledged its members ''to inflict such corporeal punishment'' on wrongdoers ''as to us shall seem adequate to the crime committed or the damage sustained.'' This, the first *lynch law,* and probably the last one written down, led to a system of kangaroo courts and, now and again, a quick hanging. Suspected criminals had been killed by impatient citizens for centuries, of course, but these hangings were the first actual *lynchings*.

After William Lynch gave the practice his name, it became as American as apple pie. Between 1882, when records first began to be kept, and today, an estimated 5,000 suspects were killed by lynchers, most of them because they were black. And there is no telling how many western innocents, like the victims in Walter van Tilburn Clark's poignant novel *The Ox Bow Incident* (1940), became guests of honor at earlier necktie parties simply because they were in the wrong place at the right time. No doubt the ''courts'' that tried all their cases used the same evidence the original ''Lynch men'' had used: they went into action ''upon hearing or having sufficient reason to believe that any species of villainy [had] been committed within our neighborhood.'' Enough to hang every neighbor in the land.

M

Macadam

In the eighteenth century many of the major roads of Great Britain were controlled by turnpike trusts, groups of entrepreneurs whose maintenance skills often lagged behind their facility in collecting tolls. A marked improvement in the condition of British highways occurred under the general stewardship of the Scottish engineer John Loudon McAdam (1756–1836). Born in Ayr, McAdam spent his young manhood in New York, making a fortune in business, and returned to Scotland in 1783, at the time of Cornwallis's surrender. Working as a manufacturer and auctioneer throughout the 1790s, he was fifty years old before he was able to turn his hobby—road construction—into lucrative employment. Paving commissioner in Bristol from 1806 on, he accepted an appointment ten years later as general surveyor for the Bristol Turnpike, then the largest trust road in the nation. The improvements he made in Bristol brought him international acclaim, and gradually he assumed control of about 1,800 miles of highway.

The *macadam,* or *macadamized,* system of construction, which was quickly adopted throughout Europe and North America, relied on a three-tiered structure of small stones, each layer tamped down first by hand, then by horse-drawn roller, and finally by passing traffic. It provided a fairly stable surface throughout the heyday of coaching, but with the advent of the automobile, which tended to jar the stones loose, macadam was gradually replaced by more compact surfaces such as asphalt.

Real McCoy

The epithet *real McCoy* to indicate authenticity has been around since the turn of the century. Lexicographers have linked it to a feud between rival branches of the Mackay clan, and to the name of a Scottish distillery whose whiskey, the "clear McCoy," was considered superior to American brands. It's true that McCoy was still being invoked as the patron of quality BOOZE in the Prohibition era, but—as Robert Cantwell shows in his excellent biography *The Real McCoy*—the original McCoy made his name not in a bottle but in the ring.

Ironically, he was not a McCoy at all. His given name was Norman Selby, and he was born on an Indiana farm in 1873. After leaving home as a teenager, he began fighting under the name "Kid McCoy" in 1891 and six years later took the world welterweight crown from Tommy Ryan. A dogged and "scientific" fighter, he made a reputation for being willing to fight anyone, anywhere, anytime, which was enhanced by a host of impersonators trading on the McCoy name. In 1899, after he scored a twentieth-round knockout against the respected heavyweight Joe Choynski, boxing writer William Naughton came up with the memorable headline NOW YOU'VE SEEN THE REAL McCOY! The phrase survived, but the Kid ceased to be a model for "the real" only a year later, when he was knocked out by Gentleman Jim Corbett in a fight widely believed to be fixed.

With his ring reputation damaged, McCoy/Selby opened a New York saloon and flirted with the infant movie industry: he appears typecast as a boxer in D. W. Griffith's 1919 hit *Broken Blossoms*. His home life was as tempestuous as his career. Married ten times (three times to the same woman), he was convicted of manslaughter in 1924 in the death of his married lover, and spent nine years in San Quentin. Upon his release he supervised security at Henry Ford's company gardens for several years and then, in

1940, took his own life. His suicide note was signed "Norman Selby."

McGuffey's Readers

What the *Dick and Jane* stories were to the children of the 1950s, the homey tales of William Holmes McGuffey were to those of a century before. Born in 1800 in then-wild western Pennsylvania, McGuffey began teaching in the rural schools of the Ohio Valley at the age of thirteen and, with a degree from Washington College, became professor of languages at Miami University at twenty-six. After serving as president of both Cincinnati College and Ohio University, he moved to the University of Virginia in 1845, where he taught philosophy until his death in 1873. In spite of this distinguished academic career, however, McGuffey's importance to American education rests solely on the six *Eclectic Readers* that he edited for elementary school use between 1836 and 1857.

The McGuffey readers, containing stories and maxims illustrating the value of piety and hard work, probably did more to spread the gospel of "moral education" than all the preachers' sermons put together. McGuffey was a champion of public education—he helped found Ohio's "common school" system, the forerunner of public schooling—and he lived to see his readers adopted as standard textbooks throughout those backwaters of the new nation from which he himself had sprung. Frequently reprinted, the six readers together sold in excess of 120 million copies.

Mach Number

Before October 14, 1947, supersonic flight was just a theory. On that day—as Tom Wolfe's book (and the subsequent movie) *The Right Stuff* recently reminded us—Chuck Yeager made it a reality. Piloting a rocket-powered X-1 aircraft, he reached that magical barrier, the "speed of sound," or (as scientists prefer to call it)

"Mach 1." Mach numbers express the ratio between the speed of a moving object and the speed of sound, so that an SST moving at thrice the speed of sound is said to be flying at Mach 3, while a plane that flies only half as fast as sound is traveling at Mach 0.5.

The Mach shorthand was named for the Austrian philosopher and physicist Ernst Mach (1838–1916), whose work in the theory of science dramatically influenced twentieth-century thought. A thoroughgoing empiricist, Mach rejected the traditional concept of an "ether," Newton's ideas about absolute space and time, and for a while, even the molecular theory of matter. A lifelong academic, he taught at the universities of Prague and Vienna, publishing books on mechanics, philosophy, and psychology that affected the thinking both of the logical positivists and of the young Albert Einstein. His association with the speed of sound comes from a relatively obscure paper on airflow which he published in 1887.

Machiavellian

For centuries this word has been used to describe political behavior that is ruthless, opportunistic, and cunning. There is some injustice in this fact. Although the Italian statesman Niccolò Machiavelli did espouse a type of realpolitik, scholars now generally agree that his fiendishness has been overstated, and that his political philosophy was that of a frustrated liberal, not the back-stabber of popular convention.

Born in Florence in 1469, Machiavelli grew up under the Medicis, that unsavory clan of power brokers who, along with the Borgias, helped to define what we mean by "Renaissance intrigue." He entered public life in 1498, four years after the Medicis were ousted by the newly formed Florentine republic; for the next fourteen years he served the republic ably, as a senior bureaucrat and roving ambassador. In 1512, aided by Spanish troops, the Medici attacked the citizen militia that Machiavelli himself had organized, defeated it, and restored themselves as the city's rulers. Arrested, tortured, and finally released, Machiavelli retired to a farm outside Florence, where he pleaded continually to be returned to public service. Except for a brief period in 1525, his hope was never realized.

In his long imposed exile Machiavelli turned his hand to writing, producing two classics of political theory. The first was *The Prince* (1513), a small, incisive "grammar of power," to use Max Lerner's good phrase, that was dedicated to a Medici and became the chief reason, then as now, that its author was associated with power politics. The second was an extended commentary on Livy's history of Rome that Machiavelli called *The Discourses* (1513–17): it defended the democratic, republican form of government and amplified an often overlooked theme from *The Prince*—that even the most "Machiavellian" leader depends ultimately on popular support. Machiavelli also found time to write a treatise on the art of war, a history of his native city, and a romantic comedy, *The Mandrake*.

It was *The Prince,* however, that made his reputation as a kind of literary antichrist—a reputation that was reinforced in 1557, when the church put his works on the Index. Machiavelli had no way of knowing, when he died in 1527, that this slim volume would become, according to Lerner, "one of the half dozen books that have done most to shape Western thought." Nor could he have known, or wanted to know, that later tyrants would take it as a *vade mecum* to justify precisely the kinds of despotism he abhorred.

Mack Truck

To be *hit by a Mack truck* is approximately equivalent, in American slang, to having the Rock of Gibraltar drop in for dinner; to be *built like a Mack truck* is to be a candidate for the Chicago Bears' line. For almost a hundred years, the German family name *Mack* has stood for sturdiness to the nth degree.

The family members responsible for the connotation were John and Augustus Mack, the middle and last of five sons born to a Pennsylvania immigrant couple during and just after the Civil War. Both left their farm home as teenagers, and after a few years on separate paths, they joined forces in a Brooklyn, New York, wagon factory run by a Dane, Christian Fallesen. When Fallesen retired in 1893, the brothers took over. Jack (1864–1924) brought his mechanical skills and Gus (b. 1873) his business acumen to a fraternal partnership that was custom-designed to meet the opportunities of the coming auto age. The brothers specialized in large vehicles, and in 1903 built the first of a very successful series of sightseeing buses for use around Brooklyn's Prospect Park. Two years later, with orders flowing in, the brothers moved their enterprise to Allentown, Pennsylvania, and incorporated themselves to manufacture "motors, cars, vehicles, boats, locomotives, automobiles, and machine and hardware specialities of every description." With that optimistic charge as a base, and in partnership with two other brothers, Jack and Gus concentrated on producing heavy-duty hauling vehicles for seven years, and then sold out their stock in 1912. Jack worked in several other automotive companies before being killed in a road accident; Gus moved to California and bought (no kidding) an ostrich farm.

Malapropism

Although the French term *mal à propos,* meaning "ill-suited," was assimilated by English writers in the seventeenth century, the use of *malaprop* and *malapropism* arose only after the success of Sheridan's first play, *The Rivals,* in 1775. The comedy's most memorable character, the aptly named Mrs. Malaprop, displays a genius for confusing similar words, and much of the play's frothy humor lies in her blundering loquacity. She speaks of the "perpendiculars" of a supposed crime. She supports a girl's need to study "geometry" so that she can understand something of the "contagious" countries. And, in one of the funnier mash notes in literature, she confesses to Sir Lucius O'Trigger, "You may be assured my love shall never be miscellaneous. Female punctuation forbids me to say more . . . yet it will give me joy infallible to find Sir Lucius worthy the last criterion of my affections." The note is signed, "Yours, while meretricious, Delia."

Mrs. Malaprop's creator, Dublin-born Richard Brinsley Sheridan (1751–1816), wrote all his major comedies while still in his twenties, enjoyed enormous popularity on the London stage, and then abruptly left the theater for politics. Elected to Parliament in 1780, he was active in government for thirty years, marking himself by his oratory in an age of such jawbone giants as Edmund Burke and the younger William Pitt. His later years were soured by debt and disease, but his funeral drew impressive crowds and he was laid to rest with his adopted country's ultimate honor—burial in Westminster Abbey.

Martial

This synonym for ''military'' comes from the Latin *martialis,* meaning ''relating to Mars.'' The most important of Roman gods after Jupiter, Mars was the god of war and, because he fathered the founders of the city, Romulus and Remus, a kind of grandfather to the Romans. Rome contained several of his temples, as well as an athletic and military drill field known as the Campus Martius; no Roman general would enter battle without first performing sacrifices in his honor.

The Romans identified him, inevitably, with the Greek god of war, Ares. They did perform similar functions, but most Greeks (the SPARTANS were an exception) never honored Ares as fervently as the Roman people honored Mars: In the *Iliad,* for example, Ares sides with the Trojans against the Greeks, and the consensus seems generally to have been that he was to be feared, but not loved.

Originally a vegetation god, Mars also protected flocks and fields. Because the fields were planted in the spring, the first month of the ancient agricultural calendar was named *Martius,* or *March,* in his honor.

Martinet

The disparaging connotation of *martinet* today is the product of an age generally suspicious of militarism, and particularly irritated by the spit-and-polish variety of which this century's goose-steppers have been enamored. The situation was different in seventeenth-century France, where Louis XIV's personal *gloire* rested as much on military expansionism as on monarchial extravagance at home. One of the men responsible for whipping the Sun King's recruits into Europe's first professional national army was the drillmaster Jean Martinet, who served as France's inspector general of infantry in the 1660s. By insisting on uniform drill and a high degree of discipline in the ranks, Martinet not only made his name a byword for MARTIAL precision but helped to set the stage for Louis's wars—wars that would continue for nearly fifty years, ravaging the continent's balance of power and creating a national debt so severe that it could only be "managed" by repudiation.

Martinet himself did not live to see this. During Louis's 1672 campaign against the Dutch, he was field marshal at the siege of Duisburg. Apparently the French artillery had not had the advantage of Martinet's training: while leading the infantry advance, he was killed by a salvo from their guns.

Typhoid Mary

A highly contagious person may be called a *Typhoid Mary* because one of the most celebrated cases of infectiousness in modern times was that of "Typhoid Mary" Mallon. Born around 1868, she was an itinerant Irish cook who was first discovered to be a carrier of the disease in 1907, after all the guests at an Oyster Bay dinner party she had prepared were admitted to a New York hospital. Authorities attempting to confine her were confounded by the fact that she disbelieved their diagnosis. Feeling fine herself, she reasoned sensibly enough that she couldn't possibly have made others ill; as a result, she broke a promise to report to health officials regularly and to refrain from working in kitchens, and for the next eight years, written up continually in the papers as "Typhoid Mary," she led the law on a wild-goose chase, with strings of fever victims in her wake. Finally cornered in 1915, she was confined in a hospital on a New York island, where she lived until her death in 1938. Counting only the reported, documented cases, over fifty people caught typhoid fever from Ms. Mallon; at least three of them died.

The Mary Mallon case was not atypical, at least in terms of the process of contagion. Food handlers are notorious transmitters of the disease; under unsanitary conditions, the typhoid bacillus, commonly excreted in urine or feces, can easily be passed from the hands of the infected carrier to the food of future disease victims. This can be prevented, of course, by stringent sanitation controls—which is why restaurant workers are now required to wash their hands after using the bathroom. The incidence of typhoid fever in this century has been dramatically reduced, not only by such commonsense precautions, but also by PASTEURIZATION, the efficient disposal of sewage, and vaccination.

In one way, of course, Mary *was* atypical. Most people who get typhoid fever recover, but only about 2 percent of them remain active carriers, that is, immune from the fever themselves but still able to give it to others. Mary Mallon was one of these anomalies—and that was the whole source of the problem.

Masochism

Masochism is the association of pleasure, particularly sexual pleasure, with abuse or pain. As a clinical term it was introduced by the German psychiatrist Richard Krafft-Ebing around the turn of the century; Krafft-Ebing's case study, and namesake, was a once popular Austrian novelist, Leopold von Sacher-Masoch (1836–95).

Sacher-Masoch was the son of a police chief, and his early years were filled with violent tales conveyed to him both by his father and by an overbearing governess whose repertory was big on torture and dominating females. A talented student and writer, Leopold earned a law doctorate at nineteen, became a lecturer in history at Graz the following year, and produced a respectable history of the Ghent uprising against Charles V when he was only twenty-one. Such academic accomplishments soon took a back seat, however, to a penchant for writing scurrilous literature, and beginning in the 1870s Sacher-Masoch turned to novels—lurid potboiling "romances" in which he evoked the sexually attractive demons of his childhood.

The typical Sacher-Masoch heroine is a large, domineering woman who lives to victimize her timid male "slaves." Sacher-Masoch worked his way toward the type in *The Legacy of Cain* (1870–77) and *False Ermine* (1873) and brought it to fruition in *Venus in Furs,* a novel that was not published until the 1890s but that was frequently reprinted and translated after his death.

Privately Sacher-Masoch was haunted by the fantasies embodied in his books. He took on a series of mistresses and two wives, dressed them all in furs like his Venus, demanded that they punish him with nail-studded whips, and encouraged them to betray him with lovers. In the early 1880s his mind went, and he was confined in an asylum until his death. He left us not only the term *masochism* but also the whole panoply of "adult" toys—Brünnhilde-type women, whips, and furs—with which the condition is conventionally identified.

Mason-Dixon Line

The line which is generally identified in American history as the official boundary between the slaveholding South and the free-state North was actually laid out in the 1760s, a century before the slavery question came to a head in American politics. Its surveyors were a pair of English astronomers, Charles Mason (1730–87) and Jeremiah Dixon (d. 1777), who in establishing the line were resolving a boundary dispute between the Penn family of Pennsylvania and the Calvert clan of neighboring Maryland. That line only later and incidentally became the North-South division.

Among eighteenth-century navigators and astronomers, Mason was moderately well known—professionally distinguished enough, in fact, to merit inclusion in the *Dictionary of National Biography*. The record of his life given there indicates an amalgam of meticulousness and wanderlust, both of which qualities were encouraged by the Royal Society. In 1761, under Society auspices, he was at the Cape of Good Hope, observing the transit of Venus. Between 1763 and 1768 he was in Pennsylvania, working on the Penn-

Calvert line and being inducted, in 1768, as a member of Philadelphia's American Society. In 1769 he was in Ireland, witnessing a solar eclipse and the late-summer comet that was later supposed to have announced the birth of Napoleon Bonaparte. In the 1770s and 1780s he was in London, publishing star charts and nautical tables that become standard in the Royal Navy. He died in 1787, in Philadelphia.

Of Dixon almost nothing is known. He accompanied Mason to Africa in 1761 and is identified as his "associate" throughout the American years. Beyond that the cautious *DNB* gives only his death date, the place (Durham), and one TANTALIZING tidbit: Dixon is "said to have been born in a coal-mine."

Mason Jar

According to the Ball Corporation, a major manufacturer of the fruit jars used in home canning, the father of the screw-top glass containers was a New York City inventor, John L. Mason. Because many of the early jars carried the embossed legend "Mason's Patent Nov. 30th 1858," *Mason jar* became a catchall term for any jar with a metal screw cap.

Mason's was not a happy history. Born probably around 1832, he opened a metalwork shop in New York in 1857, was granted his first jar patent the following year, and in 1859 began manufacturing the jars at a glassworks in New Jersey. An apparent innocent in business matters, Mason either surrendered or was finagled out of most of his patent rights, and the homemaker's boon he introduced brought him little more than folk notoriety. He died in 1902, in a New York City house of relief.

Mata Hari

Mata Hari, a Dutch-born exotic dancer, became so famous as a spy during World War I that her name ever since has been a synonym for the shadowy, dangerous *femme fatale*. Born Margaretha Zelle in 1876, she was educated in a convent, spent several years in an unhappy marriage with a Dutch army officer, divorced him, and in 1903 went to Paris to find work as a dancer. She had been stationed with her husband in Java, and she used her knowledge of that island's temple dances to create her Hindu persona "Mata Hari"—the name, she said, meant "Eye of the Dawn"—and a repertoire of highly suggestive dances, including her famous Dance of the Seven Veils. After captivating theater audiences throughout Europe, she began to specialize in private performance; the audiences were often government officials, and many of them became her lovers.

In the years before World War I the Germans, realizing the value of her political connections, sent her to espionage school, and beginning in 1914 she was spy "H21" in their service. The French secret service knew this almost from the beginning of the war, but they were hampered in apprehending her both by her own cleverness and by the implications of the scandal that would ensue if they named her French lovers without solid proof. Finally, in February 1917, possibly betrayed by her own employers, she was arrested in a Paris hotel.

Her court-martial took place in July. Because of her amorous deceptions, the prosecutor said, information had been passed to the Germans which resulted in the loss of 50,000 French lives. She was unanimously sentenced to death, and in spite of the last-ditch efforts of several lovers to save her from the firing squad, she was executed in October.

Maudlin

The British have a genius for contraction, at least in the realm of pronunciation. A popular example is the word Worcestershire, which they insist on pronouncing "Woostasheer." A less celebrated example is Magdalene, which, when it refers to the Oxford and Cambridge colleges, comes out sounding like "maudlin." But the colleges were named after Mary Magdalene, and considering her appearance in the Gospels perhaps it is not inappropriate that the contracted form of her name should evoke images of choked-back sobbing. Mark places her at the crucifixion, where it may safely be assumed that her eyes were not dry. Luke, in one of the more touching scenes in the New Testament, has her penitent before Jesus, who says of her (Luke 7:44), "She hath washed my feet with tears, and wiped them with the hairs of her head." Throughout the Middle Ages, in both the miracle plays and in painted likenesses, the Magdalene was commonly depicted as weeping; hence the connotation of *maudlin*—prevalent since the Renaissance—as "effusively sentimental."

Mausoleum

This word for a lavish aboveground tomb comes from the name of Mausolus, satrap of Caria (a province of the ancient Persian empire) in the first half of the fourth century B.C. Mausolus led a local revolt against the imperial throne in 362, captured several of the Greek islands, and established a capital at Halicarnassus, the site of present-day Bodrum. During his last years he began construction there on a massive tomb which, after his death in 353, was completed by Artemisia, the sister whom he had made his queen. This original *mausoleum*—consisting of a square colonnade, a pyramid, and colossal statuary—was widely acclaimed as one of the seven wonders of the ancient world. Although it was largely dismantled by Christian knights in the fifteenth century, the British Museum houses some remnants, including a statue of Mausolus.

Maverick

The roving gambler Bret Maverick, portrayed by James Garner in the classic 1950s television series, typified the quirky independence that we associate with this slang term. It arose in the mid-nineteenth century, thanks to cattleman Samuel A. Maverick (1803–70), who settled in Texas in 1835 and gradually acquired just short of 400,000 acres of grazing land. On a spread that size, cattle were bound to get lost, and in 1845 a Maverick herd of 400 head, neglected by a foreman, followed their noses off Sam's land and into the unfenced chaparral. When the herd's calves were born later in diaspora, they were appropriated and branded by neighboring ranchers, and from this incident any unbranded stray came to be known as a *maverick*. Gradually the term was extended to apply to anyone of an independent mind.

The Texan Samuel Maverick, incidentally, should not be confused with the Puritan settler of the same name, who had an independent spirit of his own. The Massachusetts Maverick, who came to the Bay Colony in 1624 as a young man, quarreled with church authorities over the suppression of religious liberty, going so far as to sign a 1646 petition denouncing the colony's government as an "ill compacted vessel." According to the *Dictionary of American Biography,* he was once described by a visitor as "the only hospitable man in all the Country."

Mentor

In Homer's *Odyssey,* Mentor is a trusted friend to whom the hero leaves the care of his household when he departs for the Trojan War; it is Mentor's form that the goddess Athena assumes when she accompanies Telemachus on his search for his father after the war's conclusion. The modern connotation of *mentor* as a judicious advisor, however, derives less from Homer, who uses the character only intermittently, than from the didactic epic *Télémaque* (1699), where the author François Fénelon uses the "sage counselor" as a voice for disquisitions on society, politics, and religion. A precursor of the *philosophes,* Fénelon was also tutor to the grandson of Louis XIV. The mildly liberal positions that he put in the mouth of his Mentor offended the king's absolutist sensibilities, and the writer, who was also a bishop, was forced to exchange court employment for less nettling diocesan chores.

Mercurial

The adjective *mercurial,* meaning "inconstant" or "rapidly changing," obviously refers to the metal mercury, which the Roman writer Pliny called *argentum vivum,* or "living silver," and which we know today as quicksilver. But the metal was named, in the Middle Ages, for the planet Mercury, because it moved so rapidly around the sun; the planet in turn had been named after the Roman god Mercury, because he was as fleet as the planet. Originally the patron of merchants (*Mercurius* and the verb *mercor,* "to trade," are related), he became identified with the Greek god Hermes, who was as "unstable" as the metal in two senses: as the messenger boy of the OLYMPIANS, and as the patron of tricksters and thieves. Generally depicted as an athletic young man with a winged hat and sandals, Mercury survives in commercial iconography as the emblem of Florists Transworld Delivery (FTD); considering his traditional connection to both business and speed, this is entirely fitting.

Mesmerize

All those *"mesmerizing"* after-dinner speakers have a common spiritual ancestor. He was Franz Anton Mesmer (1734–1815), an Austrian physician who, in the waning years of the *ancien régime,* made a fortune off the French as a healer in "animal magnetism."

In Austria Mesmer had proposed the existence of a pervasive and invisible magnetic "fluid" that bound together the heavens, the earth, and living matter, including human beings. By harnessing and controlling this fluid, he said, humans would be able to live longer, healthier, and more elevated lives. The Austrians saw him as a magician and forced him into exile, but as Robert Darnton shows in his small classic, *Mesmerism and the End of the Enlightenment in France,* Mesmer found fertile ground for his theories in France, where a public "intoxicated with the power of science" frequently failed to distinguish between scientific inquiry and quackery.

Mesmer arrived in Paris in 1778, bringing with him a record of cures for various ailments and a collection of metal tubs which he claimed served as transmitting media for the invisible fluid. After the French began to flock to his healing sessions, conventional and partisan scientists engaged in a pamphlet war that furthered his reputation. Mesmerist "séances," in which the master and his disciples manipulated "magnetic" areas of their (predominantly female) patients' bodies, provoked tittering and increased inquiries; eventually the enterprising doctor numbered among his champions the Marquis de Lafayette and the queen, Marie Antoinette herself. By the mid-1780s, with his Society for Universal Harmony boasting hundreds of members, Mesmer had become a wealthy man.

The mesmerist craze has often been likened to the hypnosis and spiritualist rages of the nineteenth century. In its reliance on a "black box" apparatus to concentrate ethereal forces, it also resembles this century's orgone and scientology therapies. Like orgone's Wilhelm Reich and scientology's L. Ron Hubbard, Mesmer was widely denounced as a charlatan; in 1784 he was investigated by a government commission including Antoine Lavoisier and Benjamin Franklin. Finding no evidence of a universal fluid, the commission attributed Mesmer's documented cures to psychosomatics, which, without denying their efficacy, did put a crimp in his theory.

Although mesmerism continued to exert an influence on utopian and mystical thought for decades, by 1789 its Parisian heyday was over. Mesmer left the city on the eve of the revolution, traveled through Europe for several years, and died near his Austrian birthplace just after Napoleon's fall.

Midas Touch

The ancient Greeks told two unflattering stories of the legendary Phrygian king Midas. The more famous of the two hints at the hazards of reckless choice. In this story, in exchange for a courtesy done to Dionysus (see DIONYSIAN), Midas is granted one wish. He wishes that everything he touches turn to gold, and is quickly dismayed to learn that the god takes him quite literally. The royal fingers soon aurify his food, his drink, and his daughter. Midas pleads for release from his fortune, and Dionysus allows him to wash off his magic in a stream, the banks of which ever afterward sparkle with golden sand.

In the second story, Midas judges a musical competition between Apollo, god of music, and rustic Pan (see PANIC). Ingenuously he decides in Pan's favor, whereupon Apollo gives him ass's ears. Midas hides his shame under a cap and enjoins his barber ("Only his hairdresser knows for sure") to be silent, but the man lacks the necessary control. He tattles the news into a hole in the ground, where it is heard by the reeds. When the wind flutters the reeds, the legend says, the sound we hear is the whispered secret that kings are no wiser than gods are kind.

Möbius Strip

A *Möbius strip* is the supposedly one-sided figure you get when you take a (two-sided) strip of paper, twist one end of it 180 degrees, and glue the two ends together. The resulting surface—a kind of skewed figure eight with one continuous "side"—has fascinated paradox lovers for decades, and has been especially popularized in this century by the Dutch trompe-l'oeil artist M. C. Escher.

The strip is named for its discoverer, the German academician August Ferdinand Möbius (1790–1868). Möbius was educated at home until he was thirteen, studied law and then mathematics at Leipzig, and took his doctorate there in 1814. Two years later, appointed professor of astronomy, he began a lifetime association with that university, teaching astronomy, mathematics, and mechanics; and serving after 1848 as director of the university observatory.

Möbius's writings included a classic textbook on analytical geometry (1827), popular treatises on HALLEY'S COMET (1835) and astronomical laws (1836), and an equally classic text on celestial mechanics (1843). He discovered the paper-twist phenomenon in 1858 and published the finding seven years later. Scribner's *Dictionary of Scientific Biography* points out that it was discovered independently, at almost exactly the same time, by the mathematician Johann Listing. It should therefore properly be called the Listing-Möbius strip.

Molotov Cocktail

A favorite homemade weapon among terrorists and other underdogs, the *Molotov cocktail* is a bottle filled with inflammable liquid (usually gasoline), then loosely "corked" with a length of cloth serving as fuse. The fuse is ignited, the bottle thrown, and the target, ideally, dispatched by a shower of flame. It's a cheap and lethal hand grenade, minus the SHRAPNEL, which when properly aimed can incapacitate a tank.

Most authorities agree that the incendiary device was first used in the Russo-Finnish war of 1939–40, although a minority opinion favors the slightly earlier Spanish Civil War. Whichever of these dress rehearsals for World War II deserves the credit, the device was clearly named for Vyacheslav Molotov (1890–), the Soviet foreign minister throughout the 1940s. Molotov has been credited with ordering it into production for the Soviets, but the likelihood is that the Finns came up with the name as a satirical honor for their antagonist: it was to be a cocktail *for* Molotov.

A Bolshevik ten years before the 1917 revolution, Molotov became one of the most powerful Soviet leaders in the Stalinist era. He helped to found the Communist party paper *Pravda,* headed the Council of People's Commissars in the 1930s, and negotiated the notorious Soviet-Nazi nonaggression pact, often called the Molotov-Ribbentrop pact, in 1939. His significance to the war effort is evident in the fact that he accompanied Stalin to all three of the major wartime conferences, at Yalta, Potsdam, and Tehran.

After disagreements with Stalin's successor, Khrushchev, Molotov was rusticated as ambassador to Mongolia in 1957 and five years later drummed out of the party he had helped to found. He was reinstated in 1984, at the age of ninety-four.

Monkey Wrench

The front-runners for the honor of having invented this wrench with an adjustable jaw are a London blacksmith named Charles Moncke (or Monekey) and a New England mechanic named Monk.

Of the Londoner we know nothing but the traditional attribution, and of the Yankee Monk very little more. An article in the Boston *Transcript* late in 1932 asserted, with perhaps a hint of Massachusetts CHAUVINISM, that Monk had been employed by the Springfield firm of Bemis and Call eighty years earlier and had invented the wrench in 1856. The first printed mention of the device was in an 1858 dictionary of trade products, and this sounds like corroboration of the Monk theory until you remember that the dictionary appeared in England at a time when ships, mail, and neologisms traveled much more slowly than they do today. The London blacksmith theory, on the other hand, is hampered by the fact that the English call such a wrench a "spanner." It may be that the name arose because of the tool's supposed resemblance to a monkey's jaw—or because it made the tightening of nuts so easy that even a monkey could do it.

Work saver though it was, the heavy tool could also wreak havoc with machinery if misplaced by a careless (or malicious) employee. No doubt industrial accidents were the source of our expression "throwing a monkey wrench into the works." Either that, or LUDDITE provocation.

Montezuma's Revenge

The diarrhea that attacks gringo visitors to Mexico is often called *turista* or, more pungently, *Montezuma's revenge*. The Montezuma in question was the second of two Aztec kings by that name; he has the sad distinction of having guided the Aztec empire to its destruction at the hands of Hernán Cortés and his army.

That empire had been extended throughout central Mexico in the fifteenth century, thanks in part to the first Montezuma, ruler from about 1440 to 1464. The younger Montezuma, born around 1480, came to the throne in 1502 and consolidated Aztec hegemony in the region by subduing the neighboring Tlaxcaltecas. This was to prove a PYRRHIC VICTORY, for when Cortés arrived in 1519, the subdued tribe became his staunchest ally.

The Tlaxcaltecas were only the beginning of Montezuma's problems. An indecisive and superstitious man, he was convinced by prophecies and omens that Cortés was the feathered god Quetzalcoatl returned, and so he welcomed him into his capital. The Spaniards returned this hospitality by imprisoning the king and slaughtering his subjects. In the midst of the ensuing popular revolt, Montezuma made a public plea for peace, and was nearly killed for it by his own people. He died in 1520, a year before the conquest was complete and Mexico became New Spain; it has never been clearly determined whether the Spaniards or the Aztecs did him in.

Morphine

First isolated by the German chemist F.W.A. Serturner in the early 1800s, *morphine* is the narcotic alkaloid in opium. Both in its pure form and in the derivative known as heroin, it is an extremely effective, though addictive, analgesic. It is named for the Greek and Roman god of dreams, Morpheus, the son of the god of sleep whom the Greeks called Hypnos (from which we get *hypnotism*) and the Romans called Somnus (which gives us *somnolent*). Sometimes pictured as a sleeping child, Morpheus is more commonly depicted as a winged deity carrying, appropriately enough, clusters of poppies.

Morse Code

The pattern of dots and dashes known as *Morse code* was developed by Samuel F. B. Morse (1791–1872) for use with the electromagnetic telegraph that he invented in the 1830s and first successfully demonstrated in 1844. The double invention, which Morse perfected with his business partner Alfred Vail, overnight revolutionized the art of signaling, and Morse code remained the principal method of long-distance signal transmission until well into the twentieth century.

Although Morse is remembered today solely for this achievement, in his own lifetime he was as least as well known for his artistic activities. The son of a Calvinist minister, he was educated at Yale until 1811, when he went to London to study art with Washington Allston. After a brief period of producing critically admired but unprofitable classical tableaux, he found his métier in portraiture, and beginning in the 1820s, still based in Europe, he achieved an enviable reputation for his studies of such celebrated sitters as Noah WEBSTER, William Cullen Bryant, and the Marquis de Lafayette. In 1826 he began a nineteen-year tenure as the first president of the National Academy of Design, and in 1832 he received a professorship at the University of the City of New York. We might remember him only as a distinguished American painter except that in that same year, a shipboard meeting with Charles Jackson, a student of electricity, turned his thoughts away from paints and toward circuits. Five years later he filed his first telegraph patent, and seven lean years after that he sent that famous first message—"What hath God wrought?"—from Washington, D.C., to his partner Vail in Baltimore.

Mother Goose Rhymes

Often depicted as an old woman wearing a cone hat and riding a goose, Mother Goose first appears in literature in Charles Perrault's 1697 collection of fairy tales *Histoires ou contes du temps passé* (Histories or Stories of Time Past), a book that included the classics *Little Red Riding Hood, Sleeping Beauty,* and *Cinderella.* The frontispiece of that volume showed a grandmother surrounded by children, with the subtitle *Contes de ma mère l'oye* (Stories of My Mother Goose); it was the subtitle the public remembered, both in the original French and in the first (1729) English translation.

The Perrault volume contained no nursery rhymes. Nor did a 1760 collection of stories, *The Top Book of All,* which listed Mother Goose, Nurse Lovechild, and Tommy Thumb among its "eminent authors." The old dame became associated with children's verse in 1781, when the London firm of John Newbery published *Mother Goose's Melody,* citing her as sole eminent author; since then, thousands of children's rhyme collections have been laid at her door.

Many of the ditties we call *Mother Goose rhymes* are extraneous to the Newbery book. A 1744 collection called *Tommy Thumb's Pretty Song Book,* for example, gave us "Mary, Mary, quite contrary" and "Sing a song of sixpence." *Gammer Gurton's Garland,* published in 1784, included "A diller a dollar, a ten o'clock scholar" and the Old Woman who lived in the shoe. *Melody* did have over fifty favorites, including "High diddle diddle," "Jack and Jill," "Little Jack Horner," "Jack Sprat," and the preverbal child's plum "Patty cake, patty cake." Some of these came from oral tradition, and Oliver Goldsmith (see GOODY TWO SHOES) is suspected as the author of others. What makes this an appropriate guess is the wit of the rhymes' attendant morals. The comment on "High diddle diddle," for example, is this: "It must be a little dog that laugh'd for a great dog would be ashamed to laugh at such nonsense."

Both Perrault and Newbery were notable men of letters quite aside from the Mother Goose connection. Perrault (1628–1703) championed the modernist side in the "ancients versus moderns" controversy that divided literary France in the seventeenth century. Newbery (1713–67) published Goldsmith, Samuel Johnson, many children's books, and travel narratives. The Newbery Medal, for the best American children's book of each year, was established in 1921 in his honor.

Murphy's Law

Entries in Paul Dickson's charming collection of natural (and unnatural) laws, *The Official Rules,* range from the rueful Ettore's Observation ("The other line always moves faster") to the worldly-wise Runyon's Law ("The race isn't always to the swift or the battle to the strong, but that's the way to bet"), from the staunchly practical Dobbin's Law ("When in doubt use a bigger hammer") to the whimsically cynical Canada Bill Jones's Supplement ("A Smith & Wesson beats four aces"). Dickson also provides an able discussion of the pessimist's favorite, *Murphy's Law*.

The ultimate nose-thumb to the idea of order in the universe, Murphy's Law is commonly found in its pristine form: "If anything can go wrong, it will.'' But it has spawned countless corollaries, including ''If you play with anything long enough, you will break it,'' ''If everything seems to be going fine, you have obviously overlooked something,'' and the metaphysical stunner ''Nature always sides with the hidden flaw.''

These dyspeptic bon mots were coined by dyspeptic bon mot writers at the poster companies, none of whom to my knowledge is named Murphy. The author of the original ''If anything'' line, Edward A. Murphy, was in 1949 a development engineer at the Wright Field (Ohio) Aircraft Lab. When a gauge he had designed malfunctioned that year, he traced the problem to improper wiring by a technician, and commented, ''If there's a way to do it wrong, he will.'' That offhand remark, gradually modified on the Scuttlebutt Express, was the original formulation of Murphy's Law.

N

Namby-Pamby

One person in Augustan England it was always wise not to cross was the acerbic poet Alexander Pope. Versifier Ambrose Philips (ca. 1675–1749) had the misfortune of doing just that, as a result of which his name is memorialized in *namby-pamby,* meaning "insipidly sentimental" or "indecisive." In 1709 Philips and Pope had each contributed pastorals to Jacob Tonson's *Miscellany,* and through no fault of his own Philips, a Whig, was praised in the Whig paper *Guardian* while the Tory Pope's contribution was ignored. A war of words ensued between the two poets which was to last for decades and to which a third poet, Henry Carey, was to add a memorable fillip. Carey's 1725 parody *Namby-Pamby* ridiculed the verses that Philips had written for the children of two of his friends, calling him "doubly mild, once a man and twice a child," and torturing the diminutive of "Ambrose" into the unforgettable new epithet. Pope picked up on it immediately and fastened it firmly onto Philips in the 1733 edition of his *Dunciad*—that masterpiece of satirical invective in which Philips joins laureate Colley Cibber as a minion of the goddess of dullness.

Although remembered as the butt of Pope's jokes, the original Namby-Pamby did write some respectable verse, notably in his adaptation of Racine, *The Distrest Mother* (1712). Carey wrote the popular music-hall ballad "Sally in our Alley" and also, it was rumored, "God Save the King."

Nemesis

Nemesis is commonly taken to mean any source of woe or misfortune: WELLINGTON, it might be said, was Napoleon's nemesis at Waterloo, and drink is the nemesis of the alcoholic. The more literal meaning, however, is that of disaster *deserved:* Nemesis was the Greek goddess of righteous anger, who meted out retributive justice to those whom pride or arrogance had led astray. Although artists have occasionally seen her as a personification of gentle control, the ancient stories emphasize her harsher aspects. Winged and armed, she is sometimes seen with an apple bough in one hand and in the other a wheel of fortune. It was she who caused vain NARCISSUS to fall in love with his own reflection, and who was frequently invoked as the cause of the fall of empires. In some accounts she is also seen as the ultimate cause of the Trojan War: In a curious twist on the legend of Leda and the swan, it is Nemesis who is raped by the swan (Zeus), and who gives the resulting egg to Leda. From the egg, of course, is born Helen, whose elopement with the Trojan prince Paris sparked the destruction of Troy.

Nerd

Partridge says that *nerd* became an approximate equivalent for "twit" in England around the late 1970s. This shows how slowly language may travel, even in the computer age. In the United States, *nerd* was the standard adolescent term of abuse as early as the 1950s, and at that time it meant specifically a socially inept, nonathletic "grind"; the plastic pocket-sized containers in which the tidier students held their pens and slide rules were contemptuously known as *nerd packs;* a nerd's idea of paradise was M.I.T.

In the absence of etymological evidence, I can only guess at the origin of the term. It may be related to the 1930s term *nerts,* a variant of *nuts* (for "nonsense"), but I think it more likely that the *ur*-nerd was the Edgar Bergen puppet Mortimer Snerd, a well-meaning but literal-minded hayseed who was the perfect foil to the dapper, wisecracking Charlie McCarthy. Bergen (1903–78), the most famous ventriloquist of his time and the father of actress Candice Bergen, worked Charlie on the vaudeville circuit in the 1920s and 1930s until getting a radio break from Rudy Vallee in 1936. Charlie, Mortimer, and Bergen stayed on radio for the next twenty years, and in the 1950s were frequent guests on live television. It may have been from Mortimer's TV spots that the concept of nerdiness got started.

Bergen also did several movies with his dummies, received a special OSCAR for Charlie in 1937, and was a regular on the nightclub circuit. He announced his retirement while on tour at the age of seventy-five and died in Las Vegas ten days later.

Nicotine

The active, and some would say addictive, element in tobacco, *nicotine* was named for Jean Nicot (1530–1600), a French diplomat and minor scholar who introduced the New World tobacco plant into France. As ambassador to Portugal for the French crown, he was stationed in Lisbon from 1559 to 1561. While there he received tobacco seeds from a sailor who had brought them from the Americas; after he presented them (and a quantity of snuff) to his sovereign, tobacco was named *Nicotiana tabacum* in his honor. An amateur linguist, Nicot also produced a Latin-French dictionary that was published six years after his death, and that was later discovered to be plagiarized from an earlier work.

Within a decade after Nicot's gifts, tobacco had spread across the Channel to the England of the young Elizabeth I, where it was promoted by the fashionable smoker Sir Walter Raleigh. Before long all of Europe sported pipes. Considering the havoc that smoking has visited on "civilized" lungs ever since, we may take soberly the anonymous wag's observation that tobacco, and not diarrhea, was the real MONTEZUMA'S REVENGE.

Nobel Prize

In George Bernard Shaw's 1905 play *Major Barbara,* a principal supporter of the Salvation Army turns out to be a notorious arms manufacturer, Andrew Undershaft. The ethical dilemma posed by the play—Should one do good works with "tainted money"?—was far from hypothetical at the time, because only four years earlier the first *Nobel prizes* had been given out, and if anyone was a real-life Undershaft, it was Alfred Nobel.

Born in Stockholm in 1833, Nobel moved to Russia as a boy, where he was privately tutored until he was sixteen, and where he worked in the 1850s in his father's munitions factory. He began experimenting with the recently discovered nitroglycerin in 1859, and shortly thereafter returned to Sweden, where he ran an explosives research laboratory with his brother Emil. It blew up in 1864, killing Emil, but Alfred persisted, forming the Swedish Nitroglycerin Corporation that year and a German explosives factory the next. In 1867 his persistence paid off, when he found a way to cushion the extreme volatility of nitroglycerin by imbedding it in an inert matrix. He patented the discovery immediately, calling it "dynamite."

With royalties from dynamite and other inventions, including the first percussion cap and a smokeless powder, Nobel became a multimillionaire. He constantly championed the proposition that bigger bombs were a better deterrent, but seems to have been less than thoroughly convinced of it himself: the will that established the Nobel prize fund stipulated that a fifth of the money given out each year should go to that person or group that had done the most for reducing standing armies, promoting international peace conferences, or furthering "fraternity among nations." The other four-fifths was to go to heavy hitters in areas Nobel considered crucial to human betterment: physics, medicine (or physiology), chemistry, and literature.

The approximately $8.3 million that the will put into a securities fund has been administered since Nobel's death by the Nobel Foundation. The first awards were granted in 1901, and the author of *Major Barbara* received his, for his life's work, a quarter-century later. Nobel died on December 10, 1896, and the awards have been presented ever since on the anniversary of his death.

Occam's Razor

In philosophy *Occam's razor* is the principle of economy or parsimony, often stated in the form "Entities should not be multiplied except where necessary." A recurrent theme in the writings of the medieval scholar William of Occam (ca. 1285–ca. 1349), it means basically that one should not look for complicated explanations where a simple one will do. If I slam the front door when leaving my house and find upon my return that a vase that had been on the foyer table is now on the floor, it is logical to assume that my violent exit jarred it loose. Occam's razor would cut through such unnecessarily complicated possible causes as sonic booms or earthquakes in my absence.

Born in Ockham, England, William was a Franciscan who studied with Duns Scotus (see DUNCE), wrote an important commentary on the twelfth-century theologian Peter Lombard, and for several years in the 1320s was investigated for heresy by the papal court. Taken under the protection of the French crown in 1328, he wrote religious and political treatises at the French court, where he died, probably a victim of the plague. He used his famous "razor" to limit the superfluities of scholastic discourse, and definitely not to question the influence of God in human affairs. No doubt he would have been much dismayed to find it adopted today by scientific materialists who believe that all religious thinking, by its nature, involves the multiplication of unnecessary "entities."

Ocean

The ancient Greeks imagined the world as a flat disk surrounded by the great river Ocean, beyond which lived only such exotic folk as the Cimmerians, Hyperboreans, Ethiopians, MUSES, and the blessed dead. Personified, the encompassing waters were thought of as the Titan Oceanus, son of the original Greek creation deities, Uranus and Gaia. Oceanus's dominion over the seas lasted from the Titans' usurpation of Uranus to their great war with Zeus; after the defeat of the Titans in that conflict, control of the waters passed to Poseidon (see also TITANIC).

Odyssey

An *odyssey* is a long, eventful journey. The original odyssey was the ten-year journey of Odysseus from fallen Troy to his home back in Ithaca; the term, in fact, means "Odysseus's tale." That tale, credited to Homer, was actually recited, wholly or in parts, by countless oral poets in the centuries between the Trojan War and the ninth century B.C., when Homer is supposed to have lived; many classicists now believe that "Homer" is a convenient personalization for this large coterie of anonymous singers. The text of the poem we now have was not actually written down until the sixth century B.C.

If the authorship of the poem is in doubt, not so the character of its hero. Clever, resourceful, and even devious when he must be, Odysseus is a new kind of hero: he carries not the honor-maddened ideals of an ACHILLES but the pragmatic values of survival. Some sources say that Sisyphus, "craftiest of mortals," was his father (see SISYPHEAN LABOR). Whether or not that is true, craft is what pulls him through his journey. It enables him to guide his ship home in spite of Circe and the Cyclops and the SIRENS.

Colorful impediments such as these, of course, have made Odysseus' story one of the great travelogues of all time. But the poem has always been considered far more than picaresque adventure, and Odysseus has frequently been seen as prototypically "human": he is rootless and bedeviled, but with courage and conviction he survives. The Romans called him Ulysses, and in both his Greek and Roman guises he has proved perennially attractive to writers. Tennyson's dramatic monologue "Ulysses" has the hero reminiscing as an old man. Joyce's ground-breaking *Ulysses* makes the wanderer theme part of an intensive internal odyssey. And Nikos Kazantzakis's *Odyssey: A Modern Sequel* shows, in his own words, the attempt of humanity "to find deliverance by passing through all the stages of contemporary anxieties and by pursuing the most daring hopes." A fitting tribute to this most daring of wanderers.

Oedipus Complex

Few of Sigmund Freud's theories have gained more attention, or more abuse, than his notion of the Oedipus complex—his cryptotechnical term for a pattern he perceived in many males of intense attraction to the mother and a related resentment of the father. He labeled this pattern *Oedipus complex* because in the Greek myth of Oedipus, the Theban king tragically enacts what would seem to be the logical outcome of such a psychology: he murders his father, King Laius, and marries his mother, Queen Jocasta. To Freud this myth seemed originally an expression of the ancients' own repressed desires; in *Totem and Taboo* (1918), he went further, suggesting that it portrayed, in an "artistic" disguise, a primordial communal parricide—the killing of the dominant clan father (who was keeping all the women to himself) by a "primitive horde" of jealous sons. All of religion, Freud said, was an elaborate expiation of this crime. In the absence of archaeological evidence, this story must be considered a Viennese myth. Freud's clinical point, however—that psychological health depends on resolving conflicts about one's parents—remains a valuable contribution to the discipline.

Freud, of course, was not the first to find the story of Oedipus fascinating. Numerous ancient plays were written on the theme, and Sophocles' great Theban dramas, telling the story of Oedipus and of his daughter Antigone, remain jewels of the classical tradition. In the most famous of these plays, *Oedipus the King,* we learn the tragic details of the myth. An oracle informs Laius, king of Thebes, that he will be murdered by his son; therefore, at Oedipus's birth, he gives him to a shepherd to destroy. The shepherd instead hands him over to the royal house of Corinth, where he grows up. Enter the oracle again, to inform Oedipus himself of the coming parricide. Believing that his father is the king of Corinth, Oedipus flees the city to avoid the murder—and meets Laius on the road to Thebes. They argue, he kills the king, and in all innocence marries Jocasta. When these lurid facts come to light, he puts out his eyes and leaves the city.

The Greeks understood the Theban hero not as the prototypical parricide or mamma's boy, but as a wise and noble man undone by fate. It is his wisdom, in fact, that allows him to take up Laius's throne. After killing the king on the road, he is stopped by the murderous Sphinx. She has terrorized Thebes for many years, devouring all who cannot answer her riddle: What walks on four legs in the morning, two legs at noon, and three legs in the evening? Oedipus realizes that a baby crawls, an adult walks upright, and an old person uses a cane. He replies "Man," the Sphinx kills herself, and he is welcomed into the city. Thus by lifting the curse of the monster, he rolls up the curtain on his own.

Ogre

Used today to indicate any cruel and oppressive character, the word *ogre* originally appeared in Perrault's MOTHER GOOSE tales, where it meant "a giant with a taste for human flesh." Perrault probably derived it from Italian *orco,* meaning "demon," which in turn comes from an ancient Latin epithet for the god of the underworld, Orcus. *Orcus* eventually came to be a place name for the infernal regions themselves. Its fearful connotation survives in the scientific name for killer whale, *Orca;* and in that of J.R.R. Tolkien's hobbit-hungry monsters, the hideous *orcs.*

Ohm

In 1827, the year Alessandro VOLTA died, a German physicist called Georg Simon Ohm published a pamphlet defining the basic law of electrical resistance: $I = V/R$, or current (I) equals voltage (V) divided by resistance (R). This is known as *Ohm's law* in his honor. In addition, the unit of electrical resistance is called the *ohm:* in a 120-volt circuit, for example, twelve ohms of resistance will yield a ten-AMPERE current.

Born into a family of locksmiths in 1787, Ohm spent most of his life in poorly paid teaching jobs, and was largely unappreciated in his lifetime. The British Royal Society did give him a medal for his discovery in 1841, but it was not until 1852, two years before his death, that he was recognized in his own country by being given a physics chair at the University of Munich. Later generations realized the value of his observation, and in 1893 an International Electrical Congress made the term *ohm* official.

O.K.

This most American of Americanisms arose around the time of the 1840 presidential election, when the candidates were the Whig war hero William Henry Harrison and the Democratic incumbent, Martin Van Buren. Majority opinion believes it was originally an acronym for "oll korrect," which was either a jibe used by the Whigs to insult the supposedly illiterate Democrats, or a spelling error started by former president Andrew Jackson, who had marked a pile of papers with the initials. A minority opinion, but a plausible one, says the term comes from the name of the O.K. Club in New York City, a democratic stronghold for Van Buren. One of the president's nicknames was "Old Kinderhook," referring to his birthplace, Kinderhook, New York, and club members adopted this as their title. The identification of O.K. with "all right" may have been simply a historical coincidence, as the Van Burenites raised the phrase as a campaign cry.

The first president to be born a U.S. citizen, Van Buren

(1782–1862) was Jackson's protégé and successor in the White House from 1837 to 1841. As president he attempted in vain to conciliate between factions in the growing slavery debate, prosecuted an unsuccessful war against the Seminole Indians in Florida, and presided over the disastrous financial panic of 1837. He lost the 1840 election to Harrison and ran twice more unsuccessfully. In 1844, because of his stand against the annexation of Texas, he lost the nomination, and the office, to southerner James Polk. In 1848, running on the antislavery Free Soil Party ticket, he showed a poor third behind Democrat Lewis Cass and the winner, "Old Rough and Ready" Zachary Taylor. He died at Kinderhook in the middle of the sectional conflict he had tried so hard to prevent.

Onanism

Onan, the second son of Judah in the Bible, has had a bad rap for a century because Victorian scriptural authorities interpreted his sin as masturbation, or as they liked to refer to it, "self-pollution." *Onanism* retains that meaning today, but it is based on a misreading of Genesis 38, where the young man's story appears. As careful readers can attest, the crime for which Jehovah slew Onan was not masturbation, but rather the refusal to impregnate Tamar, the widow of his elder brother Er—whom the Lord had already slain for some unspecified "wickedness." Upon Er's death, Judah had instructed Onan to marry Tamar and to give her a child which, by a quirk of custom designed to protect primogeniture, would then be raised as his dead brother's heir. Understandably, Onan balked and, instead of lying with Tamar, "spilled his seed on the ground." The Good Book does not make it clear whether this flouting of parental instruction was coitus interruptus or "self-abuse."

In any event, it was for his refusal to obey a patently prejudicial command that Onan forfeited his life. He comes down to us as a prototype of the timorous adolescent, but in justice he should be remembered as a fighter for the rights of second-borns.

Oscars

The Academy of Motion Picture Arts and Sciences was set up in 1927 to "improve the artistic quality of the film medium, provide a common forum for the various branches and crafts of the industry, foster cooperation in technical research and cultural progress, and pursue a variety of other stated objectives." Among those "other" objectives—some would say it is the Academy's only objective—is the hyping of Hollywood productions in the annual Academy Awards ceremony. Televised each spring since the 1950s, the ceremony is among our most celebrated secular rituals; the presenters' standard setup line, "The envelope, please," is more recognizable to movie-going Americans than the utterances of ministers or statesmen, and the name of the gold-plated statuettes awarded for best achievements is as well known to most of us as our own.

The prototype statuette, designed in 1928 by Academy art director Cedric Gibbons, was sculpted that year by George Stanley; it is supposed to be the figure of a knight standing on top of a reel of film. Three years later Margaret Herrick, then the Academy's librarian and later its executive secretary, remarked that it looked like her uncle Oscar. A reporter printed the observation, and the statuettes have been called Oscars ever since.

P

Panacea

The Greek god of medicine, Asklepios (the Roman Asculaepius), had several daughters. None figures prominently in ancient myths, but two did lend terms to our language. These were Hygeia and Panacea, both depicted as goddesses of health. The former, whose name means simply "health," gives us our word *hygiene*. The latter, whose name means "all healing," comes to us direct as *panacea*.

The term *panacea* today is most often invoked derisively, to chide those innocents who suppose that anything, from physical infirmity to social conflict, could admit of a universal cure. In less skeptical times, the word had positive connotations; from antiquity through the Renaissance, the search for a substance which could alleviate all ills was as serious and popular an enterprise as the quest for the Grail or the philosopher's stone. Herbalists proposed such candidates as mistletoe, balsam, mercury, yarrow, and a touch of the unicorn's horn, while throughout the alchemical tradition the mundane attempt to "change lead into gold" serves as a metaphor for a less covetous task: finding that spiritual coherence that was the answer to human confusion. The alchemists understood better than their detractors that the only real panacea lay in purity not of matter but of mind. That lesson might profitably be recalled by today's merchants of herbal magic and ginseng.

Pander

In contemporary usage, *pander* means to appeal to someone's baser nature; demagogic politicians and authors of potboilers, for example, are said to be pandering to the ignoble desires of the mob. Originally, the desires implied were sexual, and used as a noun, the word meant "a procurer of carnal pleasures," in short, a pimp. Both as noun and as verb, the word derives from Pandarus, the name of a character in Boccaccio's romance *Il Filostrato* (1344) who procures his cousin, the Greek maiden Criseida, for his friend, the Trojan prince Troilus. Both Chaucer and Shakespeare adapted the Boccaccio tale, and it is from their works that the modern English usage arose.

The unsavory connotations of the word would have surprised the ancient Greeks. Boccaccio took his character from the *Iliad,* but his Pandarus bore little relation to Homer's. The Greek poet makes him a mighty archer whose failing is a "fool's heart." It is he who, beguiled by Athena, breaks the truce between the Greeks and the Trojans by wounding the Greek leader Menelaus. Homer makes no mention of procurement, and indeed the story of Troilus and Criseida does not even appear in his poem.

Pandora's Box

Rivals in antique misogyny, the Greeks and the Hebrews agreed that evil had entered the world through the agency of the first woman. In Genesis she is called Eve; in the writings of the classical poet Hesiod she is Pandora, the "all-gifted," because at her creation all the gods, at Zeus's command, had donated something of value. Just as Eve is linked to an apple, Pandora is linked to a box, since in popular versions of the myth she is said to have carried misfortune to earth in such a vessel, which she had been warned never to open. Curiosity overcame her, she lifted the lid, and trouble was loosed upon the world, with Hope alone remaining inside. It is this story to which we refer when we speak of prying into forbidden territory as "opening a Pandora's box."

The Greek tale is marginally more conciliatory to female frailty than Genesis, for it acknowledges that the trouble really started not because of anything Pandora had done, but because Prometheus had given fire to men. No less jealous than Jehovah, Zeus worried that humans might test his power with this gift, and sent Pandora to right the balance. Why he sent Hope is unclear, although one may suppose that even such a vindictive master as Zeus would prefer to smite with a velveted hand.

One interesting sidelight: As Greek scholar Jane Harrison pointed out at the turn of the century, the original Pandora, "the beautiful mischief," actually "never had a box at all." Dora and Erwin Panofsky's iconographic study *Pandora's Box* explains that, in all the ancient versions of the story, Pandora is accompanied by a large storage jar in which, in some versions, she is enclosed. Its transformation into the small container of modern design was accomplished by no less a classicist than Erasmus, whose term for the vessel, *pyxis,* was the Latin for "box." The icon is a box to this day, in every European country but Italy, where it remains a *vaso*. And the story has been idiomatic for centuries, denoting, in the Panofskys' wry phrasing, "any source of multiple disaster from original sin to an undesirable piece of municipal legislation."

Panic

The Arcadian nature god Pan was generally portrayed by the ancients as a playful and amorous forest dweller, the maker of beautiful music and the protector of pastures and flocks. But he had an ornery side, and this led to the modern term *panic*. Depicted as a short, ungainly creature with a human torso but the legs and horns of a goat, he was thought to be fond of scaring travelers by rattling the branches of trees, shouting, or jumping out suddenly in their paths. Shepherds refrained from playing their pipes at noontime because it was known that Pan took his siesta then and would react violently against those who disturbed his rest. According to Athenian legend, the Greeks owed their victory at Marathon partly to the goat god's influence: at the turning point of the battle, he was supposed to have spread terror throughout the opposing Persians' ranks.

Although his parentage was debated, Pan was usually called the son of Hermes, messenger of the gods (see MERCURIAL). Indolent and carefree, he bears comparison both to the satyrs and to Shakespeare's mischievous Puck (see PUCKISH). Sex and music were his chief delights. This is evident in the story crediting him with the invention of panpipes. Forever in lustful pursuit of the nymphs, Pan set his eye one day on Syrinx, a mountain nymph pledged to chastity. Fleeing from him, she prayed to be turned into a reed. Her wish was granted, whereupon Pan used the reed to fashion the shepherd's rustic instrument, which musicologists still call *syrinx*. (A syrinx is also the vocalization organ in birds.)

Possibly because of his connection to shepherds and possibly because his name in Greek means "all," Pan is sometimes obliquely associated with Christ. Christian legend reports that, on the afternoon of the crucifixion, sailors at sea heard a voice announcing "Great Pan is dead." Of course this news could be read two ways. It could mean either that Jesus, the new "All," had expired, or that because of Jesus' sacrifice, the days of pagan worship were numbered.

Pap Test

The Pap test, a stain analysis technique for identifying atypical cells in cervical tissue smears, was developed by George Papanicolaou (1883–1962) and is officially called the *Papanicolaou smear test*. Born in Greece, Papanicolaou took a medical degree at Athens and a doctorate in biology at Munich. He came to the United States just before World War I, and between 1914 and 1961 held concurrent positions in pathology at New York Hospital and anatomy at Cornell Medical College. For the last three months of his life he directed the Miami Cancer Institute, which at his death was renamed in his honor.

Papanicolaou's initial research on cancer detection, done in the 1920s, got a lukewarm reception from a medical community that preferred the traditional invasive procedures of biopsy and curettage. A 1942 monograph written with gynecologist Herbert Traut, *Diagnosis of Uterine Cancer by the Vaginal Smear,* turned clinical opinion in his favor by demonstrating the value of early detection. Today the Pap test is widely accepted as a routine screening procedure and has been credited with dramatically reducing the mortality rate in uterine and cervical cancer.

Paparazzi

Celebrity-hounding photographers are called *paparazzi,* in English as well as Italian, after a particularly obtrusive example named Paparazzo in Federico Fellini's 1960 film *La Dolce Vita.* Fellini chose the name, it has been suggested, because it hinted onomatopoetically at the predatory nature of the character—a "buzzing, stinging, annoying sort of insect." Considering the voracious nature of such hangers-on, he may also have had in mind the Italian verb *pappare,* which means "to devour with wild abandon."

Born in 1920, Fellini worked as a cartoonist and story writer in Rome and then, in 1945, collaborated with Roberto Rossellini on *Open City.* After two critical flops of his own, he achieved international renown with a deft study of small-town ne'er-do-wells, *I Vitelloni* (1953). His reputation as Italy's most accomplished director was built on a string of box office hits, including four that won OSCARS for best foreign film: the neorealist masterpieces *La Strada* (1954) and *Nights of Cabiria* (1957), the utterly original, complex autobiographical fantasy *8½* (1963), and the personally nostalgic *Amarcord* (1974). In the first three of these films, as in his exuberant *Juliet of the Spirits* (1965), the star was Fellini's wife since 1943, the waifish and sensitive Giulietta Masina.

Parkinson's Law

After MURPHY'S LAW the greatest contribution to snafu science is probably *Parkinson's Law,* first pronounced in 1955 in *The Economist* by C. Northcote Parkinson. It read: "Work expands so as to fill the time available for its completion." Parkinson, an English historian based in Malaya, had spent years studying the British civil service, and his famous dictum grew out of what he saw as two "motive forces" of such bureaucracies: (1) "An official wants to multiply subordinates, not rivals" and (2) "Officials make work for each other."

His first collection of essays on bureaucratic overload, *Parkinson's Law* (1957), made the unknown professor an instant celebrity, and he has spent most of the past thirty years playing variations on his theme in new books. In spite of their bantering style, his writings are widely recognized as sound analyses of why organizations shoot themselves in the foot.

Pascal's Wager

The fragmentary *Pensées* (Thoughts) of the scientist and philosopher Blaise Pascal (1623–62) constitute a principal arsenal for Christians in their arguments with unbelievers; the Frenchman's famous wager, demonstrating the logic of believing in God, is a major weapon in that arsenal. Pascal mastered Euclid at the age of twelve, invented the first calculating machine at twenty-two, and was a pioneer in probability theory; it was to be expected that his faith would be as firmly rooted in the New Science as in traditional piety.

The wager goes like this. You are faced with the momentous decision of affirming or denying God's existence. After examining the evidence, you have come to the unwelcome conclusion that one choice is as sound as the other. You are in the position of a gambler who is in the dark about the odds and who must therefore make his bet based purely on the stakes of the game.

In Pascal's figuring (as in that of any gambler) there are two kinds of stakes. There is the stake that you put up (that is, what you stand to lose if you bet wrong) and the stake that is the prize (what you stand to win if you bet right). The rational gambler weighs these two stakes against each other, and that is what Pascal asks you to do as you debate the Ultimate Question. But, good theist that he is, he weights the scales a little, pointing out that the stakes really translate to "the Infinite" versus "Nothing." If you bet that God exists and you are wrong, all you lose is seventy-odd years of earthly existence—in Pascal's view, Nothing. If you bet that God does not exist and you are wrong, you lose the Big Enchilada—angels, salvation, or in Pascal's term, Infinity. Faced with those alternatives the choice for belief becomes, as *Star Trek*'s Mr. Spock would say, "only logical."

Pasteurization

The *pasteurization* process, which destroys microorganisms in milk and other beverages by heating, was developed in the early 1860s by French scientist Louis Pasteur (1822–95). The development was important not only in reducing deaths (especially among children) from the drinking of contaminated liquids, but also in gaining acceptance for Pasteur's germ theory of disease. Until the 1850s it had been generally believed that spoilage of alcoholic beverages was caused by the spontaneous generation of microorganisms; Pasteur's refutation of the spontaneous generation theory in an 1858 paper on fermentation is often considered the beginning of the germ theory—and of the whole science of microbiology.

A professor of chemistry and dean of the faculty of science at Lille University after 1863, Pasteur was partially crippled by a stroke in 1868, but this did not prevent him from making three other major contributions to medical theory. After identifying the anthrax bacillus, he showed that anthrax immunization was possible. He militated widely and effectively for the hygienic procedures that are now common in medical practice. And in 1885, with his use of a rabies vaccine, he laid the groundwork for research in viruses. That and other medical research continues today at the Paris-based Institut Pasteur, which Pasteur headed from 1888 until his death.

Peck's Bad Boy

A irrepressible prankster created in a series of newspaper sketches by journalist George Wilbur Peck, Peck's Bad Boy was living (though fictional) proof of two famous lines: the exculpatory adage "Boys will be boys" and Lewis Carroll's dyspeptic gibe "I am fond of children, except boys." Since the 1880s, the phrase *Peck's bad boy* has indicated an obstreperous male youngster with a nose for nuisance. A generation ago the term was as common as "Dennis the Menace," and like Hank Ketchum's charmingly troublesome Dennis, Peck's original creation was full of more mischief than malice.

Born in upstate New York, Peck (1840–1916) grew up in Wisconsin, served in that state's cavalry during the Civil War, and spent the bulk of a fruitful life in the Midwest, active in both politics and writing. An editor on various newspapers after the war, he founded *The Sun* in LaCrosse in 1874, changed the name to *Peck's Sun* and the venue to Milwaukee in 1878, and there, in a string of humorous sketches, introduced the character that made his reputation. He served as both mayor of Milwaukee and governor of Wisconsin, and became well known beyond the Badger State for such popular collections of his newspaper pieces as *Peck's Bad Boy and His Pa* (1883), *Peck's Uncle Ike and the Red Headed Boy* (1899), and *Peck's Bad Boy with the Cowboys* (1907).

Peter Principle

This often quoted principle of bureaucratic organization was first decribed in the 1969 book *The Peter Principle*. The authors, Laurence J. Peter and Peter Hull, announced brazenly: "In a hierarchy individuals tend to rise to the level of their incompetence." Their examples were drawn chiefly from the realm of higher education —for example, the brilliant classroom teacher who becomes a hopelessly inept principal.

Laurence Peter, a Canadian, was born in 1919 and has spent his professional life in the British Columbia education system. He followed the smash success of his first book with a string of amusing sequels (notably *The Peter Solution* and *Why Things Go Wrong*) that amplify the original premise. Among the apothegms that grace these works are "All useful work is done by those who have not yet reached their level of incompetence" and the gemlike "The cream rises until it sours.'' (See also MURPHY'S LAW, PARKINSON'S LAW.)

Petri Dish

A Petri dish is a small circular glass dish with raised sides that is used in microbiology laboratories for growing bacteria cultures; a loose-fitting transparent lid enables the researcher (or high-school biology student) to view the culture without disturbing or contaminating it. The simple and highly useful tool was designed in 1887 by the German physician and bacteriologist Julius R. Petri (1852–1921). He was at the time an assistant to the NOBEL PRIZE–winning bacteriologist Robert Koch (1843–1910), discoverer of the tuberculosis and anthrax bacilli.

Philippic

Like BOYCOTT and MOLOTOV COCKTAIL, *philippic* memorializes a person who did not initiate, but rather was the unwilling recipient of, the action associated with his name. In this case the ``action'' was a series of speeches, and the person was Philip of Macedon.

In 340 B.C., with his country already a major power in the eastern Mediterranean, Philip (382–336 B.C.) was threatening the sovereignty of Athens. The city-state's greatest orator, Demosthenes (385–324 B.C.), rose to the hazardous occasion by attacking aggressive Macedon and its ruler in speeches so identified with their target that the term *philippic* gradually came to be applied to any vitriolic, personal denunciation. Three centuries after Demosthenes' death, the eponym was still so well remembered that Cicero's attacks on Mark Antony were described as *orationes philippicae*.

Demosthenes, it may be recalled, was the character who put stones in his mouth to overcome a speech defect by exercising the muscles of articulation. Throughout his life he remained hostile to Philip and, after his death, to the Macedonian's son, Alexander the Great. He narrowly escaped being executed in Alexander's reign and, a year after the god-king's own death, took poison to avoid capture by Alexander's followers.

Phillips Screw

The *Phillips screw* head, in which the recess for the screwdriver bit is a cross rather than the conventional straight line, was patented in 1936 by Oregon designer Henry F. Phillips, who founded the Phillips Screw Company about the same time to market his invention. Although the greater stability provided by the cruciform recess was immediately evident to users, the initial higher cost of the screws—and the need for accompanying *Phillips screwdrivers*—kept orders at a modest level until World War II, when they proved their superiority to slotted screws in high-speed assembly-line production. The screws' popularity with defense contractors was enhanced by the company's introduction, just before Pearl Harbor, of an automatic screw driving machine that worked only with Phillips screw heads.

Phillips moved his company to New York in the late 1930s and served for several years as its first president and general manager. It is based now in Gloucester, Massachusetts, as a subsidiary of Rule Industries.

Platonic Love

Nonsexual love is often called *platonic* because in his dialogue *The Symposium,* Plato defined love as "desire for the perpetual possession of the good," suggesting that physical and temporal affections were inferior reflections of that ideal. Plato's theory of love, here and in another dialogue, *The Phaedrus,* rests on his celebrated doctrine of Forms, according to which the manifestations which humans call "reality" are in truth only shadows of the Real, that is, of a supersensible, imperishable world of truths that we can know only in fanciful approximation. This quasi-mystical doctrine had an enormous influence not only on the later,

Christian ideal of "perfect" (noncarnal) love but also on the entire range of Western thought.

Of Plato the man we know little. He was born around 427 B.C.; studied under Socrates until the latter's execution in 399; founded a school for philosophy, the Academy, which was the ancestor of the Western university; wrote a series of dialogues in Socratic form which comprise a kind of Pentateuch of Western modes of thinking; and died around 347. Plato's theory of Forms is one of the most influential concepts in the entire Western tradition. The importance of other, equally insightful, platonic ideas is suggested by Alfred North Whitehead's famous characterization of Western philosophy as "a series of footnotes to Plato."

Plutocracy

Plutocracy entered the English language in that twilight period between the Renaissance and "modern times," when mercantilism was giving way to merchant capital and the ancient hierarchies of rank and privilege were being eroded by new adventurist fortunes. The *Oxford English Dictionary* identifies the first recorded user of the term as Sir Thomas Urquhart, who in 1652 defined it as "the sovereign power of money." Given this provenance, it is understandable that nineteenth-century invocations of the word tended to associate it with the "bureaucracy" of entreprenurial administration, and that it was compared unfavorably with what Gladstone called "its elder and nobler sister," aristocracy—that is, the sovereign power of *older* money.

Young or old, the money referred to by the term was presided over in ancient times by Plutus, the Greek personification of wealth—a figure often confused with Pluto, the god of death, whose name, not so fortuitously for plutocrats, also comes from the Greek root for "riches." This etymological accident lends further confusion to the Biblical puzzle so troubling to wealthy Christians: what Jesus "really" meant when he said that it would be easier for a camel to pass through the eye of a needle than for a rich man to get into Heaven.

Greek legend says that Zeus blinded Plutus so that he would

distribute riches indiscriminately rather than with regard to merit. That sounds very much like Zeus, who could never abide just desserts. And it provides great ammunition for those who equate plutocracy with injustice.

Pollyanna

A Pollyanna will look for silver linings even when threatened by tornados. The term comes from Eleanor Hodgman Porter's 1913 novel *Pollyanna,* whose irksomely cheery heroine is devoted to what she calls the "glad game": seeking the redeeming shred of hope even in the direst of trials. In *Notable American Women,* Fred Schroeder acutely identifies the thrust of this game: "innocence and purity [bring] people with artificial reserve, with hypocritical social consciences, and with legitimate complaints about the bleakness of life all to one simple, uneducated, childish level."

Born in New Hampshire, Porter (1868–1920) studied at the New England Conservatory of Music and had earned a local reputation as a singer when, in 1901, she settled in Cambridge, Massachusetts, with her husband and invalid mother and turned her attention to writing. *Pollyanna,* her third novel, caught the affection of a public hungry for sentimental optimism, and it stayed a best-seller for two years; a sequel, *Pollyanna Grows Up,* was the fourth biggest book of 1915. Counting Mrs. Porter's own Pollyanna books and those written by others after her death, over 2 million copies were sold. The original story, widely translated, also became a stage play and two movies. America's sweetheart Mary Pickford played the title role in 1920, when she was nearly thirty herself, and Hayley Mills won a special OSCAR for the Disney version in 1960. Why SHIRLEY TEMPLE never got the part is an unsolved Hollywood mystery.

Pompadour

The upswept, top-heavy hairdo called a *pompadour* is a modification of a style popularized in the eighteenth century by Jeanne-

Antoinette Poisson, for twenty years the first lady of France. Born of an aspiring family in 1721, she was groomed from childhood in the courtly arts, and after a brief arranged marriage, became the lover of King Louis XV in 1744. Four years later he made her Marquise de Pompadour, and his *maîtresse de titre,* or official mistress. As such she wielded tremendous influence, and although historians now dispute the traditional view that she made political as well as social decisions, there is no doubt the king held her in his deepest confidence, or that, as his secretary, she was the public voice for his commands. Even after Louis took on new mistresses, she kept her apartment in Versailles and remained a decisive factor in affairs of state.

A charming and accomplished woman, Madame de Pompadour supervised a royal building program, patronized the decorative arts, arranged for the construction of the famous porcelain factory at Sèvres, and championed the authors of the *Encyclopédie* against their court detractors. The French people resented her influence, however, and held her personally responsible for the nation's involvement in the Seven Years War (1756–63), by which France lost Canada. She died in 1764, a year after the humiliating peace and fifteen years before the outbreak of the French Revolution, which brought down her royal lover's line. Her character was thus assessed by her friend Voltaire: "Born sincere, she loved the King for himself; she had righteousness in her soul and justice in her heart; all this is not to be met with every day."

Procrustean

The researcher who falsifies test results to fit a predetermined conclusion, the accountant who uses "creative financing" to balance an unbalancable ledger, the demagogue who demands unanimity of popular opinion—all may be said to be engaging in *procrustean* behavior. The word suggests a fanatic desire for uniformity, and it derives from the name of a legendary Greek villain who displayed this trait to the point of outrage.

Commonly referred to as a "robber," Procrustes might be more accurately described as a THUG, since the Greek legends do not mention him taking anything away from his victims—except their lives. He lived on the road to Athens, where he waylaid unlucky travelers and forced them to lie down on his most prized possession, an iron bed. The bed was of an exact and unvarying length, and Procrustes forced his victims to fit it in a peculiarly sadistic manner: those who were too long for the device he literally cut down to size, while those who were too short he stretched on a rack until they were right. Some versions of the story give him two beds, a long one for his short guests and a short one for the tall, hinting that his ultimate pleasure came not from the fact of uniformity but from the pain his victims suffered in achieving it.

Procrustes met a fitting end at the hands of the Athenian hero Theseus, who placed him on his own torture device and dispatched him as he had done others. The legends do not say whether Procrustes, whose name means "the stretcher," was too long or too short to survive.

Protean

In Greek and Roman legend, Proteus was a prophetic denizen of the deep whose powers, in addition to prophecy, included the ability to change his shape at will—hence the adjective *protean* for "variable" or "unstable." He is depicted generally as an unwilling accomplice to a hero who, to gain information or assistance, must hold the shape-shifter fast until he submits to be questioned. Depending on the story, this means holding on to a wild boar or a dragon, an angry lion or a flame.

Poets, for whom shape-shifting is daily work, have appreciated Proteus for centuries. He is called in by Virgil, by the authors of the medieval *Romance of the Rose,* by many Renaissance writers, and even by the minimally allusive William Wordsworth. He also figures in nineteenth-century biology. *Proteus* was an early name for the animal we now call the amoeba; and in his *Origin of Species,* that threnody for the stable, Darwin identifies as *protean* those genera which "present an inordinate amount of variation." The adjective has fallen into disuse of late, though we would profit from its restoration: few figures, real or imagined, could serve better than briny old Proteus as patrons of the weather or of politicians.

Puckish

We call mischievous behavior *puckish* ostensibly after Shakespeare's Puck, the woodland imp in *A Midsummer Night's Dream* who is responsible for most of the play's confusion. But although that Puck is the origin for the adjective, Shakespeare was actually borrowing on a long folkloric tradition in which devilish spirits called *pucas* caused trouble for unsuspecting travelers. Popular names for these sprites—who were often less fun-filled than demonic—included Robin Goodfellow, Hobgoblin, and eventually Puck. It remained for Shakespeare to give us the present connotation by muting the little demons' malice and emphasizing the mischief.

Pulitzer Prize

The Hungarian-born American publisher Joseph Pulitzer (1847–1911) was a major force in the development of modern newspaper journalism. He emigrated to the United States in 1864, fought briefly with the Union army, and in 1868 began a news career on a St. Louis German-language daily, the *Westliche Post*. His reportorial zeal made him a local celebrity, and he was elected in 1869 to the Missouri state legislature. For the next decade he juggled his political and journalistic interests until, in 1878, he purchased the failing St. Louis *Dispatch,* merged it with the rival *Post,* and produced, in the new *Post-Dispatch,* one of the country's premier regional newspapers. Pulitzer ran it until 1883, when he moved to New York to buy the paper that was to make him internationally famous: the vigorous, crusading New York *World*.

As the new publisher of the *World,* Pulitzer announced a program of editorial reform designed to make him popular with an "aristocracy of labor." The paper called for the heavier taxation of luxuries, monopolies, and large incomes; the reform of the civil service; and an end to the then common practice of employers pressuring workers at election time. At the same time Pulitzer introduced a grab bag of stunts and special features—including banner headlines, cartoons, photographs, and sensationalized treatments of crime—that were considered intemperate at the time, and that led eventually to the tabloid style that is so successful today. The demagogic vulgarisms of the paper multiplied during the circulation war with William Randolph Hearst's *Journal* that led to popular support for the Spanish-American War and to the style of reporting we call "yellow" journalism. Ironically, after that war was won, the *World* pursued an aggressively anti-imperialist policy, so angering big-stick artist TEDDY Roosevelt that the government once sued Pulitzer for libel.

Perhaps it was regret over the *World*'s occasional lapses of decorum that caused Pulitzer, in his will, to give $2 million to Columbia University. The money was to be used, he said, to establish a school of journalism and to award annual prizes for excellence in journalism and letters. The Columbia Graduate School of Journalism remains among the leading such schools in the world, and the *Pulitzer prizes,* awarded for the first time in 1917, remain the professional writer's and journalist's most coveted goal. Carrying a stipend of only $1,000 but enormous prestige, they are now granted in nineteen different categories. Pulitzer had stipulated awards in new writing, drama, fiction, history, and biography; he would probably have been pleased by the fact that the Columbia-administered honors now also go to feature writers, photographers, and cartoonists.

Pullman Car

George M. Pullman (1831–97) invented the railroad sleeping car that bears his name. Born in upstate New York, he worked there as a cabinetmaker until 1855, when he moved to Chicago to seek his fortune in contracting. He developed a prototype of the berth car in 1858, but after encountering resistance from conservative railroad owners, left for several years in the Colorado mining fields, where he ran a general store. Returning to Chicago in 1864, he perfected the sleeping car design with a friend, Ben Field, and took out the necessary patents. The first Pullman-Field car, felicitously named the *Pioneer,* was completed in 1865—just in time to become the showcase vehicle in President Lincoln's funeral train. Two years later the partners founded the Pullman Palace Car Company; with the introduction of the dining car in 1868, it soon grew into the largest railroad car business in the world.

Pullman's business practices revealed the typical contradictions of the nineteenth-century self-made man. Under his leadership Pullman, Illinois, became a model company town and the recipient of a $1.2 million fund for the establishment of a manual training school. Yet in 1897, months before its founder's death, the Pullman Company precipitated one of the bitterest strikes in U.S. history by cutting the wages of its employees but refusing to lower their rents. The ensuing violent confrontation ended only when federal troops went into Pullman and sent strike leader Eugene Debs off to jail.

Pyrrhic Victory

Pyrrhus was king of Epirus, a small country in what is now northern Greece, from 295 to 272 B.C. Throughout his reign he waged wars, first against neighboring Macedon and then against the legions of Rome. Although he was an adequate general, he purchased many of his victories at the price of such enormous casualties that ever since his day a costly win has been known as a *Pyrrhic victory.* His defeat of the Romans at Ausculum in 279 was so crippling to his own forces that he is supposed to have declared after the battle, "One more victory like this and I am lost." Seven years later he *was* lost, killed by an angry mob at Argos after having failed to conquer that city. He left behind a broken kingdom and a metaphor for ruinous success.

Players: Four From Italy

Italy's great comic drama, the *commedia dell'arte,* was created in the sixteenth century by traveling theater companies who modified the rustic folk drama of the Middle Ages to emphasize rapid slapstick action, obscene language, and general frenetic vitality. The new genre had a major impact on Europe's playwrights, including Lope de Vega, Shakespeare, and Molière, and its influence has not died out even today: the madcap spirit of the *commedia dell'arte* lives on in the films of the Marx Brothers, the Three Stooges, and Lucille Ball.

Aside from its air of naughty brio, two major elements distinguished this popular drama from the more sedate *commedia erudita* of its time. First, the *dell'arte* plays were not really "plays" at all, but elaborate improvisations on skeletal plot outlines called scenarios; the form takes its name, in fact, from the players' *arte,* or skill, in invention. Second, whatever the scenario, the improvisations were always performed by the same company of stock characters. There was always a boastful soldier named Scaramouch, for example, always a white-faced Pierrot, and always a coy, fragile Columbine.

Four of these stock *commedia* figures have left an eponymous legacy in English. First is Pantaleone, depicted both as Columbine's father and, more frequently, as a doddering Venetian merchant who is the butt of everyone else's jokes. Supposedly named for St. Pantalone, a Venetian favorite, he typically wore a robe and long tights, which came to be called *pantaloons*. Gradually the term was extended to mean any ankle-length trousers; it has now fallen into disuse, replaced by the abbreviation *pants*.

Second is the comic servant Zanni, the oldest and most important of a string of clowns who carried on most of the "business" of the *commedia* stage. Zanni is the diminutive of Giovanni. Winifred Smith, in her fine study of the genre, *The Commedia Dell'arte,* calls him "sometimes a rascal, sometimes a dunce, oftenest a complex mixture of the two, almost always the chief plot-weaver." With jokes, gymnastics, disguises, and general horseplay, Zanni could always be relied upon to keep the embers of lunacy well fanned: hence our adjective *zany*.

Eventually Zanni gave way to the *zanni,* that assortment of servant-clown figures whose numbers multiplied the chances for hilarity. Two of the most important of these clown clones were Arlecchino and Pulcinello.

Arlecchino, a genial buffoon, was often Pierrot's rival for Columbine's love. Masked and carrying a wooden sword, he was costumed in a fabric that was originally a rag pastiche, but that evolved into the multicolored pattern that gives us the term *harlequin*. As Harlequin in England and Arlequin in France, Arlecchino had a great run in pantomime.

Pulcinello, the most disreputable of the *zanni,* was also among the most popular. Sometimes stupid, sometimes cunning, frequently violent, he came to England in the seventeenth century by way of French puppet shows. Known first as Punchinello and then simply as *Punch,* he became the irascible and devious hero of the eighteenth-century Punch-and-Judy shows. In the original plot of those shows Punch murders his wife and child, is jailed but escapes, and cheats the Devil out of his soul. The supposedly mirthful mayhem of the tale has caused some to call it "Punching Judy"; our expression *pleased as Punch* refers to the character's satisfaction at escaping punishment.

Judy does not survive in American English except as a proper name, but in England it is slang for "young woman." The Beatles' 1970 hit song "Hey Jude" may be roughly Americanized as "Hey Girl."

Q

Marquis of Queensberry Rules

With minor exceptions, the rules of modern boxing matches are derived from a twelve-point code devised by British amateur athlete John Graham Chambers and sponsored publicly in 1867 by John Sholto Douglas, the ninth Marquis of Queensberry. The so-called Marquis of Queensberry rules, which ought by rights to be called the Chambers rules, included such now familiar innovations as the three-minute round with one-minute breaks, the ten-second count after knockdowns, and—perhaps most important for the modern development of the sport—the use of boxing gloves. Although bare-knuckle boxing did not really end until the 1890s, the Queensberry rules were already governing tournaments in England in the 1870s, and they have continued to do so ever since.

The marquis himself, born in 1844, served in the Royal Navy as a teenager, matriculated at Cambridge in 1864, and supported the Conservative position in the House of Lords from 1872 to 1880. According to the British *Complete Peerage,* quoting the Duke of Manchester, he was "said to have been the finest amateur boxer of his time" and was reputed to have knocked out a "gigantic cowboy" in California.

Literary buffs will know the marquis better as the father of Oscar Wilde's lover, Lord Alfred Douglas, whose association with the writer prompted the elder Douglas to accuse Wilde of SODOMY. Wilde lost both a subsequent libel suit and the government's suit against him for "gross indecency," and was sentenced to two years in prison. While there, he wrote the essay *De Profundis* and the moving testament *The Ballad of Reading Gaol,* for both of which his admirers may owe an indirect thanks to Queensberry. The marquis, the integrity of his venerable house shaken, died in January of 1900, less than a year before Wilde himself.

Quisling

The epithet *quisling* as a synonym for "traitor" or, more precisely, "collaborator" is a product of those dark days in the 1940s when Europe was under the Nazi yoke and countries with long histories of democratic process were run by governments obedient to Berlin. Although the most notorious of these collaborative regimes was France's Vichy administration, headed by Marshal Henri Pétain, it was Pétain's Norwegian counterpart, a minor military officer and failed politician named Vidkun Quisling (1887–1945), from whose name the "traitor" connotation derives.

Until he was past forty, Quisling served inconspicuously but honorably in the Norwegian army, posted throughout the 1920s to diplomatic work in the Soviet Union. He ran a famine relief program there and espoused leftist ideals, but ultimately became disillusioned with communism and, upon his return to Norway in 1930, did a complete volte-face: after a brief tenure as minister of defense, he founded Norway's National Unification Party (1933), which was devoted, like its model the Nazi party, to corporate statism and Nordic supremacy.

Throughout the 1930s, Quisling made overtures to Berlin, meeting twice with Hitler himself. Until the outbreak of World War II, he vacillated among staunch pro-Germanism, neutrality, and vague hopes for European unity. When Germany invaded his country in 1940, he became head of the puppet regime, and he served in that position, an unpopular and largely ineffective leader, until the Allied liberation. Convicted of treason by a Norwegian court in September 1945, he was shot to death the following month, protesting his innocence to the end and proclaiming, "I go to a martyr's death."

Paul Hayes, in his meticulous and evenhanded biography *Quisling* (1972), suggests that Quisling was "muddled rather than thoroughly corrupted," and that the most significant trait in his character was a "sense of dedication" to his country: "He believed that he was born to lead Norway (and the rest of the Nordic race) from darkness into light. . . . He could never understand the deep dislike which he so often aroused among his fellow countrymen."

Quixotic

The Spanish writer Miguel de Cervantes' most brilliant creation, the comically idealistic "knight errant" Don Quixote de la Mancha, has captivated world audiences for three centuries. His dogged reliance on chivalric aspirations in the middle of an infuriatingly realistic world has given us not only the adjective *quixotic* to describe any visionary or eccentric endeavor, but also the principal modern image of the "perfect fool"—that embodiment of faith against reason that a medieval audience would have applauded, but which seems so out of character for a hero today, and which is attractive for precisely that reason.

Although *Don Quixote* is among the funniest of books, its mode is tragicomedy, not farce. It is not only the elderly Don's dimwittedness—his tilting at windmills, his mistaking a flock of sheep for an army—that makes his story so endearing. Broadway viewers of *Man of La Mancha* (the musical based on Cervantes' masterpiece), like Cervantes' original audience, also see in it an addled but noble vision of human hope. Perhaps the ultimate lesson of the book is that Quixote is anything but a fool: that, in a world of mundane affairs, the only real thing *is* a dream.

The suspicion that the mundane may only be shadow might have comforted Cervantes himself, for to judge by the bare "facts" alone, his was hardly a happy life. Born in 1547, he lost the use of a hand in the army, was enslaved by Barbary pirates for five years, worked in uninspiring administrative posts for a decade, and was twice imprisoned for debt. It was probably during his imprisonment in 1597 that he began the work that was to make his reputation, but it was not until 1605, when he was approaching sixty, that the first part of *Don Quixote* was published and he achieved some fleeting financial independence. He died in the spring of 1616.

R

Rhodes Scholarships

In the will he wrote three years before his death, Cecil Rhodes provided for a fund that would enable students from the British dominions, the United States, and Germany to do two years of study, free, at Oxford University. The geographical stipulations were inevitable. All his life Rhodes had been a point man for Anglo-Saxon expansionism; a basic purpose of the Rhodes scholarships, in his own words, was to instill in the minds of young colonists "the advantages to the colonies as well as to England of the retention of the unity of the Empire." (The Germans and Americans got in, presumably, because of historical blood relationships to Mother England.) So, while it is quite right to see the Oxford plums as part of a "hands across the sea" endeavor, it is also important to remember that the program started as imperialist glue.

Rhodes, born in 1853, went to southern Africa in 1870 to work on a cotton farm. A year later he settled near Kimberley, where a recently discovered diamond field was making many Europeans rich. Rhodes became one of the richest, and the organization he founded in 1881, the De Beers Mining Company, still controls 90 percent of the world diamond trade.

With his influence growing along with his wealth, Rhodes became prime minister of Cape Colony in 1890, a year after receiving a British government charter for an ostensibly commercial organization, the British South Africa Company, that was in fact the real government of the territory. For several years Rhodes led the British assault against the indigenous peoples and the Dutch Afrikaners alike, in an attempt to realize the visionary goal of an empire "from Cape to Cairo." That dream never materialized, although he did extend his company's power over a vast area of southern Africa, including the territory once called Rhodesia (now split into Zambia and Zimbabwe). Rhodes stepped down as prime minister in 1896, wrote his famous will three years later, and died in 1902.

Richter Scale

Seismologists use two basic methods for measuring the intensity of earthquakes. One is to assess the amount of perceived destruction and to plot it on a rough continuum from "barely felt" to "total destruction." The other is to register the amplitude of the seismic waves radiating from the epicenter of the quake. This second method, which is far less subjective and less subject to localized distortions, was developed in 1935 by the American seismologist Charles F. Richter (1900–85); the scale he produced is universally used to identify the magnitude of shock waves.

It is a relative rather than an absolute scale, on which weak quakes are assigned values close to zero and each unit of measurement on the scale represents a tenfold increase in intensity over the preceding unit. An earthquake that registers at 5, for example, would be ten times as strong as one at 4, and 100 times as strong as one at 3. The scale has no theoretical upper limit, although the largest quakes yet recorded have had values no higher than 9.

Born in Ohio, Richter received his doctorate from the California Institute of Technology in 1928, worked for the Carnegie Institute in the 1930s, and in 1937 returned as a professor to C.I.T., where he spent the rest of his professional life. His publications included *Seismicity of the Earth* (1941), written with Beno Gutenberg, who also helped him refine his scale; and *Elementary Seismology* (1958).

Life of Riley

To the TV generation, the stock phrase *life of Riley* evokes memories of a shambling William Bendix, desperately trying to salvage his dignity in the face of some "revoltin' development." The affable buffoon Chester Riley, whom Bendix played in the 1950s sitcom, was the prototypical bumbling father; the joke of the series's title was that, far from leading the idiomatic life of Riley—a life of luxury and ease—poor Chester was constantly in trouble. The lesson of that quaintly charming show was that it was perfectly possible to be happy—to lead one's own life of Riley—without either money or brains.

But it was not Chester Riley whose life the idiom recalls; the phrase predates television by almost seventy years. Back in 1883, when family entertainment consisted of sing-alongs around the piano, a song-and-dance man named Pat Rooney wrote a tune called "Is That Mr. Reilly?" in which the hero, Terrence O'Reilly, dreams of wealth and position. One of the most popular songs of the "comic Irishman" genre, it had Reilly, as a rich hotelier, engineering such marvels as free railroads, an all-Irish police force, St. Patrick's Day on July 4, New York "swimming in wine," and the hero himself asleep "in the President's chair." It was in response to this song that the expression entered the language.

Ritzy

In a decade when Conrad Hilton was still in knee pants, César Ritz became the most famous hotelier in the world. Born to a Swiss peasant couple, Ritz (1850–1918) started his career, like many successful restaurateurs, as a waiter. He learned this trade in his native country, and in 1870, as Napoleon III's Second Empire was giving way to the French Third Republic, he moved to Paris. There he worked his way up into management, and in 1889, his gifts having been noticed by British visitors, he was made manager of London's Savoy Hotel. Forming his own development company, he built the first Ritz Hotel, a *belle époque* jewel on Paris's Place Vendôme, in 1898. With noted chef Georges Escoffier on his payroll, he attracted so many dignitaries to the establishment that a London investment group begged him to repeat his success on Picadilly Square. The London Ritz, completed in 1906, became the second in a chain of luxury hotels that made *ritzy* a byword for sumptuous living, and the expression *putting on the ritz* a synonym for conspicuous display.

Robert's Rules of Order

Rules of parliamentary procedure set protocols for making and debating motions and establish general guidelines for full, fair, and orderly discussion. The basic such rules used in the United States were first laid down in 1876 in a small volume called *Pocket Manual of Rules of Order for Deliberative Assemblies*. The author was Henry Martyn Robert, an army engineer who had once presided over a meeting and found himself hampered by the lack of such a guide. He based his book on the de facto rules of the U.S. House of Representatives; in revised form, and under the name *Robert's Rules of Order,* it remains the procedural bible for most U.S. deliberating bodies, from the local school board to the Senate.

Born in South Carolina in 1837, Robert graduated from West Point at twenty and a year later began his career with the Army Corps of Engineers. He supervised defense construction for Washington and Philadelphia during the Civil War, oversaw inland waterway improvements for over twenty years, and during the Spanish-American War was head of the U.S. Board of Fortifications. At his retirement in 1901 he was a brigadier general and chief of engineers. In addition to the book for which he is remembered, Robert also wrote an exhaustive index to engineering corps reports and a technical manual, *The Waterjet as an Aid to Engineering Construction*. He died in 1923.

Quick as You Can Say Jack Robinson

It is sometimes supposed that the Robinson alluded to here is the Brooklyn Dodgers legend Jackie Robinson (1919–72), who in

1947 became the first black player to break into major league baseball. Not so. The expression was common in England a century before Jackie was born. In the 1811 edition of his *Dictionary of the Vulgar Tongue,* antiquarian Frances Grose proposes a derivation that, while fanciful, is worth considering. He says the eponymous expression referred to "a very volatile gentleman of that appellation, who would call on his neighbors, and be gone before his name could be announced." Why anyone should want to do this he doesn't say, and evidently the "gentleman" never tarried long enough to be asked.

Roget's Thesaurus

Remembered as a lexicographer, Peter Mark Roget (1779–1869) was primarily a physical scientist. Born of Swiss parentage in London, he earned a medical degree from Edinburgh at nineteen, then moved south to England, where he practiced and lectured for the remainder of his long life. Although he concentrated on medicine and physiology, his interests were decidedly eclectic. His research included papers on animal and plant physiology, phrenology, GALVANISM and, for the British government, an official report on London's water supply. A fellow of the Royal Society and a founder of the Society for the Diffusion of Knowledge, he also designed a slide rule and a miniature chessboard for travelers.

Roget was in his seventies when he published the work by which he is known today. Conceived as a personal diversion, his *Thesaurus of English Words and Phrases Classified and Arranged so as to Facilitate the Expression of Ideas and Assist in Literary Composition* (1852) was an immediate success, and it has stayed in print ever since, an essential *vade mecum* for writers. Even though twentieth-century editions have been expanded considerably beyond Roget's original design, they still carry his name.

Rorschach Test

In an old joke, a patient challenges his psychotherapist: "What do you mean I've got a problem? You're the one with all the dirty pictures.'' The reference of course is to the famous Rorschach ''ink blot'' test, in which the subject is shown a series of abstract diagrams and the analyst assesses his personality based on the responses they elicit. Like all projective tests—tests in which the subject is assumed to be ''projecting'' his inner fears and frustrations on the material—the Rorschach test has been denounced as speculative and largely unreliable. Yet it is still widely used, as one of a battery of testing tools, in much personality assessment.

The test was devised by the Swiss psychologist Hermann Rorschach (1884–1921) as a way of measuring the mysterious ''unconscious'' that so excited the early psychoanalysts. Born in Zürich, Rorschach was the son of an art teacher, and as a child he was known as ''Klecks'' (Inkblot) because of his fascination with drawing. He took a medical degree in 1912 at the University of Zürich, where he worked with an early Freud champion, Eugen Bleuler. Elected president of the Swiss Psychoanalytic Society in 1919, Rorschach combined his medical and artistic interests in 1921 in the volume that introduced blot analysis, *Psychodiagnostics*. Based on his testing of hundreds of mental patients, the book also introduced Rorschach's concept of the *Erlebnistypus,* or ''experience type,'' which could be assessed, he explained, by measuring the subject's responses to the colors and ''movements'' of the inked forms.

Rorschach was married in 1910 to a Russian woman, Olga Stemplin, and shortly thereafter, while working in a Moscow sanatorium, wrote an unpublished novel about Pushkin. He also wrote on hallucinations, schizophrenia, and religious sects, but only *Psychodiagnostics* was published before his death.

Rubik's Cube

Rubik's cube, a six-sided, fifty-four-faced puzzle toy designed to be scrambled and then reassembled, hit the American market in the early part of 1981. By that summer it had become the fad of the decade. In 1982 Yale University offered a three-credit course on the cube's mathematically challenging implications; students at Illinois University built a computer that could provide solutions in two-tenths of a second; and the American television audience was treated to the finals of the first Rubik Cube Solving world championship. By 1984, when the frenzy started to die down, the Ideal Toy Company had sold literally millions of cubes, and millions more had been peddled by rival firms under different names.

The person responsible for the madness was Erno Rubik, a teacher of architecture and design in a Budapest school for commercial artists. He had developed the cube in 1974 as an instructional aid for applied arts and patented it in Hungary three years later. He did not patent it in the United States, however, and his oversight gave corporate lawyers a field day. Throughout the early 1980s Ideal defended its own patent on the toy against companies that had copied it successfully and were marketing it more competitively. Then, in the summer of 1982, Ideal found itself on the other end of the suit business, when a Cambridge, Massachusetts, company called Moleculon claimed that its chief research scientist, Larry D. Nichols, had patented a similar item in Moleculon's name back in 1972—and had been refused a marketing contract from Ideal. In 1984 a federal judge hinted that the toy ought really to be known as Nichols's Cube by ruling in Moleculon's favor. A $60 million damages lawsuit against Ideal was pending as of this writing.

S

Sadism

Sadism is clinically defined as a sexual perversion in which pleasure can be obtained only through the infliction of pain on another. Thus, according to an old joke, a sadist is someone who is kind to a masochist. Unfortunately, it's not that simple. In probably the majority of cases, sadistic acts illustrate an arrested sexual development linked to a need to exert control over an unwilling victim. This has certainly been the case historically, whether the sadist is a rapist, a Nazi, or the member of a Central American hit squad. It is evident in those contemporary "entertainments" known as slasher movies, and it seems to have been true as well in the case of the French literary MAVERICK who gave us the clinical term: the "divine" marquis, Comte Donatien Alphonse François de Sade.

Born in 1740, the Marquis de Sade received a Jesuit education, served in the army during the Seven Years War, and married money at the age of twenty-three. Five years later, however, the course of his life changed dramatically when he was jailed for torturing a prostitute. For most of the next fifty years, he scandalized France by his riotous behavior—including the attempted poisonings of other prostitutes—and was more often in prison than out. As anyone who has seen Peter Brook's extravagant play *Marat/Sade* will remember, he died in the lunatic asylum at Charenton. The end came in 1814.

De Sade would have been dismissed as a mere psychotic had it not been for his lubricious literary skill. His first novel, *Justine,* written in prison and published privately in 1791, expanded on the conventions of the "wronged maiden" that Samuel Richardson's *Clarissa* had started; with its graphic descriptions of the heroine's mistreatment, it became the model for *Police Gazette*–style romances and garnered its author a ready audience of such enlightened libertines as Danton. Further treatments of the theme appeared in *Philosophy in the Bedroom* (1795), *Juliette* (1797), and the posthumously published *One Hundred Days of Sodom* (see SODOMY).

A mere cult figure in his day, de Sade was rediscovered in the nineteenth century and was particularly admired by such brilliant fringe writers as Baudelaire, Swinburne, and Cocteau. In her charming survey *Sex in History,* Reay Tannahill wonders why: "Whether this was because the bloodied horrors of his imagination fed some private need in themselves, or whether it was because he had emptied a metaphorical slop-bucket over the outraged head of bourgeois respectability, has never been entirely clear." It remains unclear today.

Saturnine

This synonym for "gloomy" or "depressed" refers to the Roman god Saturn, who was about as close to being a patron of melancholia as GOODY TWO SHOES or POLLYANNA. In ancient astrology the *planet* Saturn was thought to have a baleful influence on human affairs because of its sluggish motion and its extreme distance from the Sun (it was the farthest known planet at the time). It was entirely inappropriate, however, to have named this bearer of bad tidings after the god, for Saturn—even though he was later identified by the Romans with the grim Greek creation god Cronus—was preeminently a god of good cheer. He was believed to have brought farming to Italy, and founded a long-vanished Golden Age. At his annual festival, the Saturnalia, this Golden Age was briefly reenacted: prisoners were freed, war ceased, gifts were exchanged, slaves were waited on by their masters, and a general air of merriment prevailed. This popular December celebration (later assimilated by the church into Christmas) was the least saturnine time of the year.

Saxophone

The saxophone is best known today for its versatility as a jazz instrument. It was created, however, to be used by French military bands. Its inventor was Antoine Joseph Sax (1814–94), the most successful member of a Belgian family of instrument makers. A clarinet virtuoso, Sax developed his namesake woodwind by indirection, in trying to improve the clarinet's tone: the saxophone combines the clarinet's single reed with the bore and fingering pattern of the oboe.

After study at the Brussels Conservatory, Sax went to Paris in 1842, with what Groves's *Dictionary of Music* calls "no capital beyond his brains and fingers." The support of Hector Berlioz and others enabled him to buy tools and hire artisans, and in the 1844 French exhibition he won the first of many medals for his work. With his eyes on supplying the French army, he patented two trumpetlike instruments in 1845: the *saxhorn* and the *saxotromba*. Together with the *saxophone,* patented the following year, they so enchanted the army brass that Sax was given the monopoly he had hoped for: his creations replaced the traditional oboes and bassoons, and the sound of the modern marching band was born.

In spite of his technical and marketing skills, Sax had no head for business. The honors and money he pulled in—culminating with the Grand Prix at Paris in 1867—could not save him from frequent reverses, and in the 1870s he was forced to sell both his business and a huge collection of his instruments. His most famous creation was little used by classical composers, and he died without seeing its tremendous impact on popular music.

Great Scott!

This exclamation most likely invokes the American military leader Winfield Scott (1786–1866), who ably commanded troops in the War of 1812, the Black Hawk War of 1832, and the Creek and Seminole conflicts of 1835–36 before becoming general in chief of the army in 1841. In the war against Mexico, which began in 1846, Scott was in charge of the amphibious landing at Veracruz and the capture of Mexico City. He became so popular by these exploits that he was a serious presidential candidate on the Whig ticket in both 1848 and 1852. In the latter year he became the party's nominee, and it was during the election campaign that *Great Scott!* probably got started: it's not clear whether it was a term of respect invented by supporters or a jibe created by detractors who believed that "Old Fuss and Feathers," always a stickler for discipline, was finally getting too big even for his own britches. In any event, Scott lost to Franklin Pierce. He reentered public life a decade later, when at the outbreak of the Civil War he was put in charge of the forces defending Washington; he resigned shortly afterward, at the age of seventy-five.

Scrooge

Scrooge as an equivalent for "miser" comes of course from Charles Dickens's justly beloved story *A Christmas Carol* (1843), in which the principal character is the tightfisted merchant Ebenezer Scrooge. The story, which Dickens himself loved as fervently as have generations of readers, presents Scrooge as a stiff-necked, merciless coin-counter, completely insensitive to the plight of the poor, who is eventually converted to "the Christmas spirit" by the lessons of three seasonal ghosts: the Ghost of Christmas Past, who shows him his own carefree childhood; the Ghost of Christmas Present, who shows him the straits into which his parsimony has driven the family of his employee Bob Cratchit; and the Ghost of Christmas Yet to Come, who predicts obloquy and oblivion for Scrooge if he does not reform his ways. Scrooge does reform, becoming a model of good cheer and philanthropy. Yet his name remains a byword for stinginess.

Although *A Christmas Carol* is still widely read, the Scrooge character has probably reached more people through television than Dickens, or his publishers, could ever have envisioned. Alastair Sim's 1951 interpretation remains the definitive version; Albert Finney in 1970 and George C. Scott in 1984 commendably updated the classic role.

Scrooge of course was only one of a huge cast of Dickensian

characters to have gripped the fancy of the English-reading public. Others with eponymous legacies were the type of the sniveling hypocrite, *David Copperfield*'s Uriah Heep; and *Martin Chuzzlewit*'s Seth Pecksniff, from which we get *pecksniffian,* for "sanctimonious."

Sequoia

California's giant redwood trees, also known as sequoias, were classified as genus *Sequoia* by the Hungarian botanist Stephan Endlicher (1804–49). Since he was also an ethnologist, it has been traditionally assumed, although it is not strictly provable, that he chose the name in honor of Sequoyah, the Cherokee Indian figure credited with the invention of the only known Indian "alphabet," the eighty-six-character Cherokee syllabary.

Born in 1770, Sequoyah was the son of a Cherokee mother and a white trader, Nathaniel Gist or Guess. An accomplished hunter and trapper, he was lamed in an accident as a young man and turned his attention to more sedentary pursuits, among them silversmithing and languages. After learning French, Spanish, and English, he set about adapting the Europeans' system of "talking leaves" to the peculiarities of the Cherokee tongue, and in 1821 first demonstrated his invention to his people: legend says he convinced the elders of the written word's power by having his six-year-old daughter read to them a message they had dictated to him out of her hearing. In 1822 he introduced the syllabary to the western Cherokee in Arkansas, and six years later, as the federal government was just starting to consider removal of the southeastern tribes, Sequoyah accompanied them to Oklahoma. Once there, he became a tribal leader, served as an envoy to Washington, and started the first Indian language newspaper, the *Cherokee Phoenix*.

If Sequoyah had hoped that literacy would give his people greater bargaining power with the whites, he was sadly mistaken. In the spring of 1838, the last of the southeastern Cherokees were taken from their ancestral homes and farms and force-marched to arid Oklahoma; on the infamous Trail of Tears, over one third of the 13,000 died. Sequoyah left the survivors himself in 1843, traveling west to seek a legendary lost band of his people who had left the southeast before the Revolution. He died in Mexico shortly thereafter. Oonoleh, a Cherokee who went searching for him in 1845, sent a letter back east in Cherokee characters, announcing the aged leader's death and burial, and reporting that "Tsusaletah, the son of Sequoyah, remains on Red River. He is very sorry that the remains of his father are buried so far from his own country."

Shlemiel

The Yiddish *shlemiel* is consistently unlucky, slow-witted, and/or all thumbs. He opens the refrigerator door and the eggs fall out. He just makes the train going in the wrong direction. Or, in a folk proverb quoted by Leo Rosten, he "falls on his back and breaks his nose." *Shlemiel* humor is to Jewish culture what the moron joke used to be to American culture: the history of a well-meaning loser.

Of the several examples cited in Rosten's wonderful book *The Joys of Yiddish,* one illustrates especially well the *shlemiel's* combination of earnestness and incompetence. Two *shlemiels,* Rosten says, were drinking tea. One announced portentously, "Life is like a fountain." The other asked him simply "Why?" The first thought for a moment and sighed. "So O.K.: Life *isn't* like a fountain."

Rosten suggests two eponymous sources for *shlemiel*. One is German writer Adalbert Chamisso's 1814 story *Peter Schlemihl,* in which the hero sells his shadow to the Devil and is plagued by ill luck ever after; the commonest meaning of *shlemiel* in Europe is still "anyone who makes a foolish bargain." The other is the Jewish general Shelumiel, a supposedly incompetent field commander mentioned in the Book of Numbers. These are worthy, but dubious, guesses. Numbers says nothing, one way or the other, about Shelumiel's battle achievements, and the Chamisso story is too recent to have generated the traditional term. What the story probably did was to broaden the usage of an expression already common in Jewish folklore.

Sideburns

A century before Elvis thought of growing them, sideburns were the rage throughout America thanks to a Civil War general named Ambrose Burnside. Born in 1824, he graduated from West Point in 1847 but resigned his commission in 1853 in order to manufacture a rifle he had invented, the quite successful Burnside carbine, at a factory in Bristol, Rhode Island. With the outbreak of war in 1861, he returned to service, commanding his first brigade at Bull Run. Made a major general in 1862, he then led a checkered career. After performing competently, if not brilliantly, at Antietam, he became head of the Army of the Potomac, presided over the costly Union defeat at Fredericksburg, and was swiftly removed from his command. Transferred to the Army of the Ohio, he saw action in 1864 at the Wilderness, Petersburg, and Cold Harbor.

A stolid, imposing figure with deep-set eyes and a dramatically receded hairline, Burnside sported thick black side whiskers which came to be called Burnsides, and then, by transposition, *sideburns*. His personal charm and appearance evidently impressed voters more than the Fredericksburg disaster did, because after the war he served three terms as Rhode Island's governor and six years in the United States Senate. He died at Bristol in 1881.

Silhouette

The David Stockman of his day, Etienne de Silhouette was both respected and reviled in prerevolutionary France as an architect of austerity. Born in 1709, the son of a tax collector, he moved slowly through the provincial bureaucracy until, at the age of fifty, he was noticed by Louis XV's mistress Madame de POMPADOUR and elevated to the position of minister of finance. This was in 1759 when, unfortunately for Silhouette, the Sun King's various extravagances were beginning to send birds home to roost.

The fiscal crisis he had inherited from a century of budget-straining *gloire* Silhouette confronted in a novel fashion: he sought relief not only from the Jacques in the street but also from the nobility. Among the parsimonious measures advocated in his administration were the cutting back of aristocratic pensions and the elimination of trouser cuffs. Because of the latter suggestion cuffless trousers became known as *culottes de Silhouette* and the man's name itself became a synonym for "cheap."

The painting and cutting out of what we today call *silhouettes*—outline portraits, usually of human faces—had been a popular folk art in Europe since antiquity. Until the invention of photography, it attracted numerous hobbyists, among them Silhouette himself. It is uncertain, however, whether the word's current usage arose because of the minister's avocation or because of his vocation of cutting back to essentials.

Sisyphean Labor

Sisyphean, meaning "frustrating and endless," comes from the Corinthian king Sisyphus, whom Homer calls the craftiest of mortals—crafty enough to cheat death twice. The first time, ordered into the underworld by Zeus for having revealed one of his intrigues to a jealous husband, he manages to lock Hades in his own manacles, so that for several days no one can die—including himself. The second time he arranges for his wife to give him an improper burial, and has to go back to set things right. When he dies for the third and last time, he is sent to Tartarus, where he has to roll a boulder up a hill. This becomes the first Sisyphean labor, since every time he reaches the top it tumbles down past him again. Camus uses the story in *The Myth of Sisyphus* (1942) to illustrate the absurdity of human existence.

Sopwith Camel

Whenever Charles Schultz's *Peanuts* character Snoopy takes to the air against the Red Baron, the airplane he flies is a *Sopwith Camel*. Snoopy's craft may be imaginary, but the Sopwith Camel was real. One of the most famous of World War I fighter planes, it was a small, fast, single-engine biplane developed in 1917 by a British firm, the Sopwith Aviation Company, which had been founded five years earlier by Thomas Sopwith.

Born in 1888, Sopwith was an extraordinary airman in his own right. In 1910, after teaching himself how to fly, he won the de Forest prize for the longest flight from England to the Continent; in 1912 he won his nation's first aerial DERBY; two years later he took home the Schneider trophy for a seaplane built after his design. During World War I his firm supplied the Royal Flying Corps with thousands of the highly maneuverable aircraft that held the skies over France against the German Fokkers. The Cuckoo model was the first plane to drop a torpedo. The Pup was the first to take off and land from a carrier. But it was the Camel that made Sopwith a household name: far and away England's most successful fighter, it accounted for nearly 1,300 enemy kills.

For his contributions to the war effort, Sopwith was made a Commander of the British Empire in 1918. In the 1930s he was twice an unsuccessful challenger for yachting's America's Cup. Knighted in 1953, he makes his home in the south of England.

Sousaphone

The instrument that most of us call a tuba—that huge-belled, oom-pah-pah monstrosity—is strictly speaking not a tuba but a helicon: to the musicological purist, tubas have vertical, straight bells, and helicons have spiral (that is, helical) ones. Since helicons were developed in the nineteenth century for use in marching bands, it is not surprising that the American version of these spiral "tubas" was built for, and named after, the American "March King" himself, John Philip Sousa (1854–1923).

Initially trained as a violinist, Sousa played with the U.S. Marine Band as a teenager, left to conduct and play with symphony orchestras in his twenties, and returned as the Marine Band's leader in 1880. After twelve years with them, he formed his own marching band, which for the next twenty years was the brassy toast of two continents. In addition to his over one hundred marches—which included the perennial favorites "Washington Post" and "Stars and Stripes Forever"—Sousa also wrote dozens of songs, fifteen operettas, the autobiography *Marching Along* (1928), and three novels.

Spoonerism

The Rev. William Archibald Spooner (1844–1930) was an ordained Anglican priest, a moderately distinguished scholar, and for fifty years an Oxford college don. All of this is forgotten because of his supposed penchant for metathesis. Metathesis is the transposition of sounds within a word ("drat" becoming "dart") or from one word to another (a grocer asking a customer if he wishes to "fry some boot"). The latter kind of metathesis is what we today call a *spoonerism*.

A prime example of Spooner's quirk is the tirade he is supposed to have delivered to a troublesome undergraduate: "You have tasted a whole worm. You have hissed my mystery lectures. You were fighting a liar in the quad. You will leave by the town drain." Vintage stuff, to be sure, but as Spooner's respectful biographer, Sir William Hayter, observes, like many other "authentic" spoonerisms it is far too complex a comic utterance to have been a mere *lapsus linguae:* reason spies a pundit's invention. Hayter cites a few genuine slips, such as the reverend speaking of the Flood story as being "barrowed from Bobylon," and misquoting I Corinthians so that we see "through a dark, glassly." But he discounts the celebrated errors, such as the announcement of the hymn "Kinkering Kongs" and the allusion to a "half-warmed fish"; and he gives not even a passing nod to his subject's most famous supposed blunder: the description of Queen Victoria as "our queer old dean."

Not that Spooner was crystal clear. Hayter acknowledges his occasional social blundering. He once apologized to a New College visitor that he would not get a chance to meet Mrs. Spooner—while his wife was standing beside him. After preaching a full, mystifying sermon, he paused to inform his student audience, "In the sermon I have just preached, whenever I said Aristotle, I meant St. Paul." And there is the "acted spoonerism" described by historian Arnold Toynbee. Having spilled salt at a dinner party,

Spooner reached for a bottle of wine, tilted it meticulously over the spill, and turned the dry salt a soggy crimson.

Spooner was slight, shortsighted, and albino. At least one physician has suggested his confusions were related to dyslexia, and perhaps to albinism too. In any event, Spooner's problems did not prevent him from taking two firsts at New College, serving as its warden for twenty years, and producing a respected edition of Tacitus. As the salt on the table tale suggests, he may simply have been cagier than he showed. Certainly some of his confusions, in Hayter's words, were "full of point." When the Indian mystic Krishnamurti, touted as an avatar of Christ, applied for admission, Spooner regally announced: "I understand that Mr. Krishnamurti is supposed to be an incarnation of Our Lord, so of course we can't have him at New College." And, when he punctured a dinner partner's hand with a fork, he replied, "Madam, I believe that's my bread." Perhaps he merely had a why drit.

Stetson

In the iconography of the movie Western, only the horse and the COLT .45 are more significant than the high-crowned, broad-brimmed *Stetson* hat. John Wayne wore a Stetson. Gene Autry wore a Stetson. Everybody from William S. Hart to Clint Eastwood—whatever the developing wrinkles of the genre—has remained true to that original image: the man on the horse with the hat. The urban cowboys who mimic the image today on Saturday nights in Pasadena would no doubt be surprised to learn that the Stetson, no less than the Colt, was a product of the decadent East.

Its creator was John Batterson Stetson (1830–1906), the son of a New Jersey milliner who, after apprenticing to his father, lit out for the Colorado gold fields during the Civil War. Like TEDDY Roosevelt he went West largely for his health, and like LEVI Strauss he found among the far-flung prospectors a gold mine for his own mercantile talents. Returning East in 1865, he opened a hat factory in Philadelphia, specializing in a fixed-price line designed to appeal to the Western tastes he had noted in his travels. His wares proved enormously popular. By the time of his death, his Philadelphia factory was producing 2 million hats a year, and the Stetson had become as much a part of cowboy fashion as chaps or Levi's or bandanas.

Like Strauss, Stetson was a model employer. His 3,500 workers enjoyed savings and benefit funds, stock options, and a regularized bonus system long before American industry in general caught on to the seemingly obvious notion of "productivity through people"; with George Eastman (Eastman Kodak) and Samuel Johnson (Johnson Wax), he suffered the slings of unionists who were convinced that his "benevolent feudalism" was a mask for subtle oppression. He was also a model philanthropist, liberally funding a university near his winter home in DeLand, Florida; it still bears his name today.

Svengali

A *Svengali* is one who exercises a mysterious and/or inordinate influence over another; quack therapists and Eastern gurus are often so characterized in the press. The prototype was the villain of *Trilby* (1894), a once very popular novel by the English writer George du Maurier. The heroine, a young model named Trilby O'Ferrall, falls in love with an English art student but is deflected from the romance when she meets the Hungarian-born Svengali, a sinister musician who controls her singing voice through hypnosis and transforms her into a star. When he dies, she loses in quick succession her voice, her career, and her life.

Du Maurier (1834–96), once an art student in Paris like Trilby's hapless lover, was a successful caricaturist for *Punch* and also illustrated works by Thackeray, Hardy, and James. His novel *Peter Ibbetson* (1891) was made into an opera by Deems Taylor. His granddaughter was Daphne du Maurier, best known for her romance *Rebecca* (1938).

T

Taj Mahal

India's Taj Mahal, an exquisite jewel of white marble and precious stones, is often called the most beautiful building in the world. Certainly it is the most beautiful MAUSOLEUM. It was built between 1632 and 1643 to honor the memory of the Mughal Shah Jahan's beloved wife, who had died in 1631 while bearing him a fourteenth child. Her name was Arjunand Banu Begum, but she was known by the honorific title Mumtaz Mahal, which means "Crown of the Palace"; *Taj* is a corruption of *Mumtaz*. Jahan, who became emperor of India in 1628, lived to see the completion of this masterpiece of architectural symmetry and died in 1658. He was buried alongside his wife beneath the edifice that bears her name. No doubt they would be astonished to learn that that name is now carried not only by the building but also, as a stage name, by the American blues singer Henry Fredericks.

Tantalize

To *tantalize* someone is to offer him or her something at once desirable and unattainable, such as a mechanical rabbit to a racing hound, or moral perfection to humans. The verb derives from Tantalus, a legendary Lydian king. Son of Zeus and preferred to all other mortals by the gods, Tantalus is said to have invited the OLYMPIANS to a feast at which the main course was his own son, Pelops, in a stew. The king's motives for the act were unclear. Some believe he wanted to demonstrate his subservience to the immortals, like Abraham in the Bible. Others imputed to him simple malice, hubris, or a yen for macabre jokes. Whatever his reasons, the gods were not amused. Discovering the atrocity, they condemned him to an eternal and peculiar punishment.

Forced to stand in the underworld in a pool of clear water, Tantalus was forbidden ever to drink, for every time he bent down to slake his thirst, the water drained into the ground. And even though clusters of fruit hung from branches apparently within his reach, he was also forbidden to eat: every time he extended his hand, the inviting branches were blown out of range by a divine wind. Thus he was made to stand forever, in his frustration a companion victim to Sisyphus (see SISYPHEAN LABOR).

Pelops, meanwhile, was restored to life by the gods and, as spouse to the mortal princess Hippodamia, sired a line of celebrities that kept the playwright Aeschylus in business. His most famous son, Atreus, founded the notorious "house of Atreus," which energized both the Trojan War and Aeschylus's Oresteia trilogy (see ELECTRA COMPLEX). Another son, Pittheus, was the grandfather of the hero Theseus, the legendary king of Athens who was known for his defeat of, among others, Procrustes (see PROCRUSTEAN) and the Minotaur.

Tawdry

Tawdry, meaning "poor in quality and taste," is a contraction of "St. Audrey," in turn the Normanized form of "St. Etheldrida." Etheldrida, or Audrey, was a seventh-century East Anglian princess who founded a religious house in Ely and was for many years its abbess. She died of a throat tumor, and was reported (by no less venerable an authority than the Venerable Bede) to have thanked God on her deathbed for the affliction, seeing it as recompense for her frivolous youth, when she had been partial to heavy gold necklaces. Centuries after her burial at Ely, merchants established an annual fair in the vicinity, and at this fair lacemakers sold strips of their finery which, worn by Renaissance women as "neck laces," were known as "St. Audrey's lace." Whether this term predated or followed the fairs is uncertain. What is clear is that, as "tawdry" came gradually to be applied to mementoes other than lace, Etheldrida became the hidden patroness of anything shabbily ornamental.

Teddy Bear

In the two terms he served as America's twenty-sixth president, Theodore Roosevelt (1858–1919) earned a well-deserved reputation as a tough customer. "Trust Buster" Teddy enacted a campaign to reform corporate abuses with the same vigor and determination that made his foreign policy a model of no-nonsense imperialism. Yet he had a soft spot, as well as a soft voice, behind the big stick, and this characteristic was ironically responsible for the creation of his namesake, the *teddy bear*.

In November 1902, the president, an active sportsman, was bear hunting down in Mississippi. Members of his party captured a bear cub and brought it to Teddy to shoot. Either out of simple kindness or because he saw an opportunity for good press, he ostentatiously refused to do so. Reporters filed the story, and a couple of days later Clifford Berryman, a cartoonist on the *Washington Post,* depicted the presidential gesture as "Drawing the Line in Mississippi"—a pun on the fact that Mississippi and Louisiana were then involved in a border dispute. A New York candy-store owner, Morris Michtom, then got the bright idea of manufacturing small stuffed "Teddy Bears" to capitalize on the cartoon. The president gave him permission to use his name, Michtom and his wife, Rose, started sewing, and in 1903 an American tradition was born.

Among teddy bear collectors, the most valuable models are those produced in the early 1900s by the doyenne of European bear-makers, Germany's Margarete Steiff. But the Michtoms' Brooklyn-based enterprise did not fare badly either. The venture they founded on a cartoon grew into Ideal, one of the major toy companies of this century. (See also RUBIK'S CUBE.)

Thespian

The old-fashioned term *thespian,* for an actor or actress, comes from the name of the Greek poet Thespis, commonly acknowledged as the first individual actor and the father of Attic tragedy. He lived in the sixth century B.C., during the tyranny of Peisistratus, whose public building programs and encouragement of the arts in Athens were contributing to a growing civic unity. Before Peisistratus's time, Greek drama consisted of unorganized rural festivities in honor of the god Dionysus (see DIONYSIAN); the tyrant brought these celebrations into the city, built a theater on the Acropolis, and paved the way for the community dramas of the next century. Thespis's contribution was to transform the traditional choral structure of the celebrations into something approximating dialogue; he won first prize in a citywide poetry competition in 534 B.C. and about this time became the first "star" performer by stepping forward from the chorus and reciting alone. Building on Thespis's daring innovation, Aeschylus, two generations later, added a second individual actor, reduced the role of the chorus, and produced the first great tragedies.

Tupperware Party

Since World War II, the *Tupperware party* has become as much an institution of suburban America as the barn dance and the quilting bee were of rural life a century before. An amalgam of sales conference and kaffeeklatsch, the typical Tupperware gathering enables housewives not only to trade casserole recipes but also to do what the Tupperware company hostess expects them to do: place orders for the plastic household containers on which the company's hundreds of millions of dollars in annual sales revenues depend.

Both the containers and the party concept were developed by a canny Yankee salesman named Earl S. Tupper. Born in New Hampshire in 1907, Tupper grew up on a Massachusetts farm, sold produce as a boy, worked in the mail-order business as a young man, and toward the end of the Depression began experimenting with plastic. After developing a flexible, heat-resistant material he called poly-T, he started his own company in 1942, and within five years was doing $5 million in annual sales. At about the same time he initiated the housewives' distribution network through which Tupperware products are still exclusively sold. By the time he was ready to hand over the management of his firm to the Rexall Drug Company in 1958, he was able to sell it for $9 million.

Tupper continued to serve as chairman of the board of the Rexall subsidiary until 1973, when he retired to Costa Rica. At the time of his death there in 1983, his party concept involved a quarter of a million part-time "dealers" in thirty countries. Together these Tupperware hostesses throw approximately 75,000 parties a year.

A Brief Tome on Tom

Next to JOHN and JACK, historically the given name *Tom* seems to have been among the most popular in the English language. In nursery rhymes (which might be expected to reflect common tastes in baby-naming), Tom appears continously. In my daughter's edition of MOTHER GOOSE, I find not only the familiar *Little Tommy Tucker* and *Tom the Piper's Son,* but also *Tommy Snooks*—who gets in because he rhymes well with Bessie Brooks—and another Little *Tommy,* this one surnamed *Littlemouse,* about whom it is said that he "lived in a little house" and "caught fishes in other men's ditches." In the Renaissance we get *Tommy Thumb,* a diminutive nursery-tale hero whose name P. T. Barnum later appropriated: his discovery, the midget entertainer Charles Stratton (1838–83), toured extensively as *General Tom Thumb.*

None of these nursery Tommies has infiltrated the common idiom. Not so with a number of other Toms. The *Doubting Thomas* of the Bible has become a patron saint of the skeptics; this is from a mention in John 20:25, where Thomas, of the sanctified twelve apostles, will not believe that Jesus has risen from the dead until he can put his finger into the print of the nails that had held Him to the cross. The *Peeping Tom* of medieval legend has become a byword for prurient unrestraint. It was he who spied Lady Godiva on her uncovered Coventry ride and was blinded as a reward. The *tomfool* of modern *tomfoolery* is also a medieval invention: the earliest mention in the *Oxford English Dictionary* is 1337, where this archetypal prince of inanity is spoken of as *Thomas Fatuus,* or "Thomas the Silly."

Tomboy is a Renaissance word. Early in the sixteenth century, according to the *OED,* it meant a "rude, boisterous, or forward boy." By the end of the century it is being applied to young women too, when they violate female decorum. Another century on we find *tomcat,* playing like tomboy on the propensity to identify *tom* with "male." WEBSTER's even today sees it as a prefix for any species, although tomcat, *tom turkey,* and tomboy are the only real survivors of this usage.

Tom, Dick, and Harry is nineteenth century, a nonlegalistic variant of John Doe. Eric Partridge records a curious history of this "man in the street" designation, beginning with combinations of Jack, Tom, Tib, Dick, Harry, and Will in the seventeenth century; moving through Tom and Dick in the eighteenth; and passing from Tom, Jack, and Harry in the mid-nineteenth century down to the current arrangement. Another nineteenth-century generification is simple *Tommy* or *Tommy Atkins,* the British military John Doe, from the name commonly printed on enlistment forms.

The more modern usages of the name are easier to track down. UNCLE TOM comes from the novel that hastened the shots on Fort Sumter. The TOMMY GUN, or "Chicago violin," was invented by U.S. army officer John T. Thompson. *Tom Collins* is an American corruption of John Collins, the British public-house owner who is credited with the drink's invention. *Tommyrot,* from the turn of the century, may have come from the British soldier's ire at being issued *tommy* (goods, or bread) rather than wages. And the obscure but ingenious *tommyrotic* was coined by a Chicago art reviewer in 1895 to deride the then current notion that "progress in art requires the elimination of moral ideas."

U–Z

Uncle Sam

Army recruiting posters since World War I have popularized the image of *Uncle Sam* as a lean, goateed gentleman in a top hat and swallowtail coat. The artist for those posters was James Montgomery Flagg (1877–1960), who used himself as a model to revise a figure originally created by Gilded Age cartoonist Thomas Nast (1840–1902). But the idea of Uncle Sam as a personification of the United States government is much older than Nast's cartoons.

The most popular explanation for the origin of Uncle Sam is that it was the nickname of Samuel Wilson (1768–1854), a Troy, New York, army provisions inspector during the War of 1812. According to legend, one of Wilson's workmen, seeing the initials "US" on a packing case being shipped to the army, surmised aloud that they must stand for "Uncle Sam" Wilson—and the conjecture stuck. This charming bit of folk etymology, although informally recognized by Congress in 1961, has more wit than substance. As long ago as 1908, in the *Proceedings* of the American Antiquarian Society, Albert Matthews debunked it on several counts.

The Wilson story, Matthews pointed out, was not told in print until 1842, three decades after the packing case incident was supposed to have taken place. Although the term *Uncle Sam* first appeared in a Troy newspaper in 1813, the story did not make the connection to townsman Wilson; nor was it made in contemporary books about Troy, or even in Wilson's own obituaries. Matthews's mundane but reasonable conclusion was that *Uncle Sam* was a jocular expansion on the initials that, long before 1812, had stood for "United States." The first printed reference to Uncle Sam, in fact—the 1813 Troy story—specifically suggests that the term arose from the letters on government wagons. With or without Sam Wilson, the term rapidly gained currency in a nation which, racing after Manifest Destiny, needed its own version of JOHN BULL.

Uncle Tom

When Stokely Carmichael and other black militants in the 1960s called the followers of Martin Luther King *Uncle Toms,* they were reiterating a gibe that had first been leveled years before at the followers of Booker T. Washington. To the radical wing of the black protest movement, Washington and King always seemed accomplices in oppression—Washington because of his emphasis on education rather than political activism and King because of his Christian propensity for turning the other cheek. The father figure of the militants, W.E.B. DuBois, expressed the antagonism to *Tomism* well when, in an essay on Washington, his contemporary, he called the conciliatory educator "a compromiser between the South, the North, and the Negro" and attributed to him "the old attitude of adjustment and submission."

If *Uncle Tom* retains its strength as a rebuke, however, it is due less to the passions of this century than to the impact on popular thinking that was effected by the original Uncle Tom—the kindly, Bible-quoting "happy darky" created by Harriet Beecher Stowe (1811–1896) and made the sentimental protagonist of her influential antislavery novel *Uncle Tom's Cabin.* Published in 1852, the book portrayed Uncle Tom as a dutiful, saintly servant who is repaid for his goodness by being beaten to death by the drunken slave master Simon Legree. As unfair as the attribution of compliance may have been to the civil rights leaders of this century, it is hard to deny that Stowe's prototypical Uncle Tom was a thrall to "adjustment and submission."

Stowe herself, although born and raised in Connecticut, had at the time of her famous book's publication lived for a decade in Cincinnati, on the border of the slave state Kentucky. She was also the daughter of the abolitionist minister Lyman Beecher, so her attack on the horrors of slavery should be seen as a complex amalgam of observation, outrage, and church piety. Frequently cited as a "cause" of the Civil War, *Uncle Tom's Cabin* might more accurately be described as the kindling that had long been awaited for a smouldering bed of coals.

Valentine

Two Saint Valentines gave their name to the February 14 lover's day, and neither one had anything to do with romance. Both lived, according to Christian legend, in the third century; both were priests martyred by beheading in Rome; and both had their feast day on February 14—at least until the Church, in a fit of post–Vatican II historicism, took it off the liturgical calendar in 1969. That is about all we know of them. The name Valentine became associated with romantic love because of two quirky coincidences. A major Roman fertility festival, the Lupercalia, occurred on February 15; and a long-standing folk tradition said that birds began to pair off for spring nesting on February 14. In honor of one or both special days, lovers exchanged gifts and murmurings about the middle of February each year. The martyred Romans were assimilated into this tradition, and before long missives of devotion became known as *valentines* in their honor.

Vandyke Beard

The *Vandyke,* or more properly Vandyck, beard is a short, well-groomed beard that comes to a sharp V below the chin. It was briefly popular during the beatnik era of the 1950s, and before that in the 1890s. The style was named for the Flemish painter Sir Anthony Van Dyck (1599–1641), whose portraits of British and European aristocrats reflect its popularity in his day.

A native of Antwerp, Van Dyck studied with Rubens as a teenager, established a glowing reputation as a portraitist during a tour of Italy in the 1620s, and in 1632 was called to England to become court painter to Charles I. Knighted shortly thereafter, he produced elegant, sensitive portraits of the nobility and royal household that brought him enormous success and, in 1639, marriage to Lady Mary Ruthven. His sensitivity to the personality of his sitters and his use of darkly rich Italianate coloring moved English painting away from its customary stiffness, giving it a suppleness that would soon be evident in the work of Gainsborough and Sir Joshua Reynolds.

Always frail, Van Dyck died after a brief visit to the Netherlands and France in 1641. He left behind him, in addition to his portraits, a number of notable religious scenes and a reputation second only to Rubens's.

Volcano

Volcanos are named after Vulcan, a destructive fire god in ancient Italy to whom the Romans, in one of their queerer rituals, sacrificed live fish once a year. His violent characteristics are later muted, after he comes to be identified with the saddest and cleverest of the OLYMPIANS, the Greek fire deity Hephaestus.

A lame and ugly god, Hephaestus is the son of Zeus and Hera. Some legends say he was born lame, others that he acquired the affliction after being hurled from heaven by one or both of his parents. In any event he is an outcast from Olympus, and generally despised by the gods, even though, in a wonderfully ironic touch, he is also married to the immortals' beauty queen, Aphrodite (see APHRODISIAC).

Hephaestus's supreme gift is his hands. With Athena he is patron of the crafts and, thanks to his association with fire, is specifically the god of the forge. The gods may turn from him, but not from his works. These include the armor that protects ACHILLES outside of Troy, Zeus's scepter, and the figure of the first woman, PANDORA. Because of his skills and ingenuity, Hephaestus is the founder of material culture, and thus to a certain extent of civilization.

Hephaestus/Vulcan is also remembered in the term *vulcanization,* for the process of strengthening rubber by heating it; and in the name of the fictional planet *Vulcan,* home to a race of culturally advanced beings whose most famous former inhabitant is *Star Trek*'s unflappable Mr. Spock.

Volt

Electrical energy sources produce a type of energy known as electromotive force. Conventionally measured in *volts,* this force may range from the 1.5 volts of a typical flashlight battery, through the 120 volts of most home wiring systems, to the many thousands of volts that course through overhead power lines. The measure *voltage,* as well as the unit *volt,* are named for Alessandro Volta (1745–1827), one of the pioneers of electrical theory.

An Italian physicist, Volta was a gymnasium teacher in Como when, in 1775, he invented the electrophorus, a device for transferring electrical charge to other objects. Between 1776 and 1778 he successfully isolated methane gas, and in the latter year he became professor of natural history at the University of Pavia. It was while teaching at Pavia that he performed the experiments by which he is chiefly known. Attempting to prove Luigi Galvani's theory of animal magnetism (see GALVANIZE), he undermined it instead, by discovering an electrical charge external to animal tissue, created by the contact between different metals. To study this type of charge more completely, he constructed a pile of metal disks which, to the delight of the scientific community, generated a continuous electrical current. This self-charging "Voltaic pile," invented in 1796, was the prototype of the dry-cell battery. Edward Canby, in his stimulating *History of Electricity,* calls it "the greatest of all electrical discoveries." To honor his discovery, Napoleon made Volta a count in 1801. He retired from Pavia in 1815, and died twelve years later.

Watt

Power output is measured in *watts,* whether you're talking about a 100-watt light bulb or a hydroelectric dam with a half-million kilowatt capacity. It is entirely fitting that this basic unit of power should have been named for James Watt, for no individual did more than this unassuming Scottish inventor to drive the wheels of the Industrial Revolution. Born into a successful builder's family in 1736, he was trained as an instrument maker, and was practicing that trade at the University of Glasgow in 1757 when a meeting with physicist Joseph Black turned his attention to steam thermodynamics. At the time, a steam engine developed by Thomas Newcomen was being used throughout the British Isles to pump water out of coal mines; it was his improvements on Newcomen's design that earned Watt the imprecise title "father of the steam engine."

Watt's first and most significant design change was a 1769 condensation chamber that dramatically improved the engine's efficiency. Five years after patenting this invention, Watt entered what was to be a twenty-six-year partnership with the Birmingham manufacturer Matthew Boulton. With Boulton's commercial intelligence and Watt's mechanical fecundity—he also designed gears, other engines, and a governor for automatic speed control—the partnership was immensely successful. By the end of the century virtually every large factory on two continents was humming along on Watt's version of steam power. And a "traditional" term which Watt himself had coined, *horsepower,* was gradually giving way to his namesake.

Watt retired, a wealthy man, in 1800 and settled down to a busman's holiday at his home. Fitting his attic out as a workshop, he continued to tinker and invent, producing among other things a "sculpting machine" which reproduced busts and figurines. A member of the Royal Society since 1785, he accepted a doctorate from Glasgow in 1806 and a place in the French Academy of Sciences in 1814. Modesty prevented him from accepting a baronetcy offered by the crown.

Watt died at home in 1819 and was buried beside his longtime partner, Boulton. A statue of him stands in Westminster Abbey.

Webster's Dictionary

That *Webster* has become almost a shorthand equivalent for "dictionary" is due less to the considerable success of the Merriam-Webster Book Company than to that indefatigable front man for the American language, the revolutionary lexicographer Noah Webster. Born in 1758, Webster taught school and practiced law as a young man, but he showed an early interest in the American idiom and set out in the 1780s to correct what he saw as the young nation's slavish attitude toward British-dominated publishing. The result was his *American Spelling Book,* which did much to standardize American spelling and sold more than 60 million copies by the end of the century.

In 1787 Webster moved from his native Connecticut to New York, where for the next fifteen years he managed various magazines with a strong Federalist flavor. In 1803 he turned from political writing to devote his full attention to lexicography, producing his first dictionary in 1806. His second effort, finished in 1825 and published in 1828, was *An American Dictionary of the English Language,* which the *Dictionary of American Biography* calls "probably the most ambitious publication ever undertaken, up to that time, upon American soil." In including nonliterary terms and "Americanisms," Webster furthered his design of producing a comprehensive survey of the indigenous idiom, and the work earned a quick, and richly deserved, reputation on both sides of the Atlantic.

The cogency of Webster's magnum opus was a result at least in part of its author's enormous range of interests. In addition to language and politics, he produced various treatises on economics, a two-volume study of epidemics, a learned edition of Puritan father John Winthrop's journal, and a number of pioneering studies in climatology. He also worked actively for the reform of copyright laws and was a founder of Amherst College in Amherst, Massachusetts, where he lived for several years in midlife. After 1822 he lived in New Haven, where he died in 1843.

Mae West Jacket

The inflatable life jackets that saved so many airmen and sailors from drowning in World War II were called, even before the war began, *Mae West jackets* or just *Mae Wests*. The reason was coarsely obvious. They bulged "in all the right places," just like the buxom screen actress who so captivated audiences in the 1930s that, by the middle of that decade, she was the highest paid woman in the United States. The term began as a serviceman's jest, but by the early 1940s, in both the British and American forces, it had become official.

Born in Brooklyn in 1892, the redoubtable Miss West made a name for herself even before World War I, when on the vaudeville and burlesque circuits she was billed as the "Baby Vamp." Her first play, *Sex* (1926), caused such an uproar in New York that the police had to close it down and place West (who wrote, produced, and directed it) in jail for obscenity. In *Diamond Lil,* two years later, she became a national star, and soon moved her talents to Hollywood, where she reprised her Diamond Lil role (opposite Cary Grant) in the eyebrow-raising film *She Done Him Wrong* (1933). Subsequent films—notably the 1940 *My Little Chickadee,* with W. C. Fields—entrenched her sultry reputation, made her the darling of female impersonators, and gave the American idiom such timeless one-liners as "Beulah, peel me a grape" and "Come up and see me sometime." Her 1959 autobiography, echoing another famous quip, was entitled *Goodness Had Nothing to Do with It*.

The enduring quality of West's ironic sexiness was demonstrated in 1970, when in the idiotic film *Myra Breckenridge* she made an eerily graceful comeback. Eight years later, at the age of eighty-five, she make a final screen appearance in the appropriately named comedy *Sextette*. She died in 1980, leaving behind an eponymous legacy that at one time included not only the life jacket but also a double-turreted tank, a billowing sail, and a cruller with a figure-eight design.

Zephyr

To the ancients, Zephyr was the personification (in some tales the god) of the West Wind. It was he who killed HYACINTH rather than surrender him to Apollo, but the act was highly uncharacteristic: Zephyr was consistently depicted as the mildest of the four winds, as soothing as his comrade Boreas (see AURORA BOREALIS) was wild. Poets in antiquity summoned him into serene tableaux, and by the Renaissance, disguised as the lower-case *zephyr,* he had become a stock piece in lazy afternoons—the inevitable accompaniment to fluttering heartbeats and grasses.

Today the once revered West Wind, like the crinoline and the quill pen, has been buffeted into near obscurity by a markedly unsentimental age. But in the nineteenth century the term *zephyr* did extra duty. To Keats and other romantics, it continued to mean the soft breeze of classical tradition; in common prose it also meant any lightweight article of clothing, a genus of butterfly, and a type of soufflé.

Zeppelin

The dirigible (steerable) airship was invented by Frenchman Henry Giffard in 1852; the rigid dirigible, in which the balloon is given integrity by a metal framework, was developed much later in Germany, under the direction of Count Ferdinand von Zeppelin (1838–1917). Zeppelin was commissioned in the German army in 1859, fought with Union forces in the U.S. Civil War, and made his first balloon ascent while exploring the Mississippi River. He served in the Franco-Prussian War, attained the rank of general, and upon his retirement in 1891 devoted himself to airship design. In 1900, after piloting the first successful rigid model, he founded the Zeppelin Company, which was to produce over one hundred more such craft in the next thirty-six years. After World War I proved them too vulnerable to gunfire for military use, the company turned to the civilian market. Among its most famous ships were the luxurious *Graf Zeppelin,* which made dozens of Atlantic crossings in the 1930s; and the equally luxurious but ill-fated *Hindenburg,* whose explosion at a New Jersey mooring dock in 1937 effectively ended the zeppelin craze.

Although the zeppelins are gone, their smaller, nonrigid cousins the blimps are still with us. They are called "blimps," incidentally, not after the interwar cartoon figure Col. Blimp, but because the British and American armed forces designate these frameless models as "Class B—limp."

Strictly speaking, an eponym is derived from an individual person's name. But since groups of persons (whether they are nations or Rotary Clubs) also have names, here is a representative list of "collective eponyms"—terms that reflect the real or supposed characteristics of more than one eponymous individual.

Amazon

An *amazon* is a tall, athletic woman, often thought to be hostile to men. In Greek mythology the Amazons were a nation of women living near the Black Sea in Asia Minor. Isolated from the world of men except for battle and procreation, they trained their daughters as warriors and killed or enslaved their sons. The name, which means "without a breast," refers to their supposed practice of cutting off the right breast so it would not hinder their pulling a bow. It was the ninth labor of Hercules (see HERCULEAN TASK) to secure the girdle of their queen, Hippolyta; he managed to kill her in the process. Another queen, Penthesileia, was killed in the Trojan War by ACHILLES, who upon removing her war helmet fell in love with her—instantly but still too late. The Amazon River was so named because its Spanish explorer, Francisco de Orellana, was attacked there in 1541 by skirted Indians that he took to be women.

Assassin

The original *assassins,* like many of their modern counterparts, hailed from the Middle East. Members of a Shiite Muslim sect that flourished in the twelfth and thirteenth centuries, they terrorized both the Crusaders and the orthodox Muslims in power. Marco

Polo and others reported that their murders were frequently preceded by the ingestion of hashish; thus they came to be called "hashish eaters"—in Arabic, *hashshashin*.

Banshee

To scream or wail like a banshee, now an all-purpose simile for any ruckus, originally meant to mourn for the dead. The *shee* were the fairy folk of old Ireland, and a *banshee* was a female of the breed. When a banshee's cry was heard outside a window, it meant someone in the house would soon die.

Beggar

Although the etymology is uncertain, *beggar* may derive from "Beghard." The Beghards were thirteenth-century lay mendicants, a group founded by the priest Lambert de Bègue. An undisciplined, wandering fraternity, they antagonized medieval Church leaders because of their populist bias and their closeness to female Béguines. The leaders may have had cause: modern French gives *béguine* as "Flemish nun" and the expression *C'est mon béguin* as "He [or she] is my darling."

Cynic

The Cynics were ancient Greek philosophers who displayed that disdain of given wisdom and worldly pleasures that the conventional label bizarre. They acquired the appellation *kynikos* (doglike) because they met at the gymnasium Silver Hound—or perhaps because they were thought of as dogs. The most celebrated of the group was Diogenes (c. 404–320 B.C.). He wore rags, slept in a tub, and carried a lantern in search of an honest man. Calling himself Athens's one free man, he was the first to *épater le bourgeois*. Alexander the Great once asked Diogenes whether he could do him a favor; he was told, "Stand out of my light."

Dervish

A *dervish* in Persian is a Muslim monk, usually of a mendicant order. In English idiom all dervishes continually dance or whirl, but the characterization is actually true only of the more mystical sects. Chief among them today are the Sufis, who engage in ritual choreography to bring about a trancelike calm.

Gothic

Among the Italian Renaissance artists who coined it, *Gothic* was a term of reproach: it implied that, compared to classical buildings, the medieval cathedrals were so crude that only a Goth could produce them. In indirectly condemning the Goths, they were reviving an ancient anxiety, for it had been the southward migration of these German barbarians, in the fifth century A.D., that had hastened the decline of ancient Rome. Under their leader Alaric they had sacked the city itself in 410, and so they were frequently coupled with the VANDALS as paragons of blind, destructive rage.

Gyp

The dark-skinned nomads known as *gypsies* entered Europe from India in the Middle Ages, and have been stereotyped and maligned ever since. Frances Grose gives the stereotype vividly in his *Dictionary of the Vulgar Tongue* (1811), when he calls them "a set of vagrants who, to the great disgrace of our police, are suffered to wander about the country . . . and, under the pretence of fortune-telling, find means to rob or defraud the ignorant." Thus *gyp* means "to swindle or cheat."

Laconic

Laconia is that section of Greece inhabited in ancient times by the SPARTANS. Trained to be soldiers, not orators, they were known throughout the Greek peninsula as a people of few and choice words: that is, as *laconic* folk. Willard Espy gives a charming example. A would-be conqueror sent a warning: "If I come to Laconia, not one brick will stand on another." The Spartans' reply was "If."

Lesbian

The term *lesbian* to mean female homosexual refers directly to the Greek island of Lesbos and indirectly to that island's most famous daughter, the poet Sappho (b. 612 B.C.). Vilified for centuries because of her impassioned lyrics to other women, Sappho has become in this century a priestess of lavender feminism. Scholars dispute her sexual proclivities but agree on at least two things: she ran a kind of salon for Lesbian (not necessarily lesbian) young women, and her poetry is first-rate. The ancient Greeks agreed with this too. They spoke of her as the tenth MUSE.

Lilliputian

Jonathan Swift wrote his 1726 masterpiece *Gulliver's Travels*, also known as *Travels into Several Remote Nations of the World*, in four parts. In the first, his voyager, Lemuel Gulliver, visits Lilliput, whose inhabitants are six inches tall. Certainly the best remembered of the acerbic wit's four "remote nations," it survives in *lilliputian*, meaning "tiny."

Muse

A single concept underlies our words *muse, music,* and *museum*. It is that of the Muse, or more properly Muses, who inspire all arts of the mind. According to the eighth-century Greek poet Hesiod, the Muses were the nine unnamed daughters of Zeus and Mnemosyne (or Memory, from which our *mnemonic*). Later Roman writers gave them names and specified areas of expertise:

Calliope (epic poetry), Clio (history), Erato (lyric), Euterpe (music), Melpomene (tragedy), Polyhymnia (religious song), Terpsichore (dance), Thalia (comedy), and Urania (astronomy).

Olympian

WEBSTER gives one meaning of *Olympian* as "a being of lofty detachment or superior attainments"—an idiomatically accurate definition which, considering the shenanigans of the Mt. Olympus crowd, is a lie of Olympian proportions. These quite fallible Greek deities were Zeus, Hera, Poseidon, and Hestia, all siblings; and the eight children of Zeus: Aphrodite, Athena, Hebe, Artemis, Ares, Apollo, Hermes, and Hephaestus. Olympian is not to be confused with *Olympic:* the athletic games started in Olympia, nearly 200 miles from Mt. Olympus.

Philistine

The Philistines were Israel's most implacable foes in Biblical times, harassing both Samson and Saul before being subdued by King David. Their name survives in modern *philistine,* meaning a materialist, uncultured BABBITT, because of a town-and-gown brawl and a sermon. According to the *Oxford English Dictionary,* in 1693 in the German college town of Jena, a student was killed by a townsman, and the minister who preached his funeral chose the text "The Philistines be upon thee, Samson"—Delilah's false warning to her lover after she has had his head shaved. *Philistine* immediately became a student term for all those not part of the university, and gradually its meaning was broadened to encompass anyone disdainful of education.

Puritanical

Puritanical today suggests a crabbed paranoia about sex—a cast of mind supposedly common among the Puritans of the seventeenth century. I have questioned this supposition elsewhere (see my *Fabulous Fallacies*), but it's true that the Puritans honored marriage and that they saw the human body as a vessel for not only joy but temptation. They also had a much wider program than is hinted at by Hawthorne's *Scarlet Letter*. The original, English Puritans desired nothing less than the complete scouring of "Romish" influences from the Anglican church. Their followers emigrated to America, in fact, feeling Elizabeth I had not gone far enough in wiping BLOODY MARY's legacy from the realm.

Pygmy

We get our modern word *pygmy* not from the central African Pygmies but from mentions in classical literature. Homer spoke of a short-statured people living on the shores of great OCEAN, and Herodotus wrote of one in Africa: they called them Pygmies for the Greek measure *pygme,* the distance from the knuckles to the elbow. Homer's story was myth, and since Herodotus was notorious for telling tales, no one took him seriously either, until nineteenth-century explorers proved him right. These explorers gave the Greek name to the newly discovered short tribes.

Siamese Twins

Congenitally joined identical twins are called Siamese because the most famous historical examples were the brothers Chang and Eng Bunker (1811–74), who were actually three-quarters Chinese but did come from Siam. Since they shared liver tissue, they could not be separated safely, and for several years their condition made them a popular carnival attraction; they were squired around the country by P. T. Barnum. After 1843, however, they led remarkably normal parallel lives: they married twin sisters, settled on a North Carolina farm, and between them fathered twenty-two children.

Siren

An enticing or seductive woman is called a *siren* because the Sirens of Greek mythology lured sailors to death on the rocks with the enchanting sweetness of their song. Only two heroes slipped their net: Jason, whose companion Orpheus sang a sweeter song than the Sirens; and Odysseus, who—warned by Circe that he would be passing the Sirens' rock—plugged his crew's ears with wax and had them bind him to the mast (see also ODYSSEY).

Slave

Slavery is as old as "civilization," but the first form of the word *slave* recorded by the *Oxford English Dictionary* is the Greek *sklavos* in the sixth century A.D. In Greek and then in borrowed Latin it referred to the Slavs of eastern Europe, who in the early Middle Ages were frequently "reduced to a servile condition by conquest." The extension to any servile person was accomplished by about 900.

Sodomy

Generally construed to be any "unnatural" sexual act, *sodomy* is variously defined, depending on local laws, as oral sex, anal intercourse, bestiality, and/or homosexual sex in general. In the United States, a homophobic bias often informs such legislation: as of this writing, five states (Arkansas, Kansas, Montana, Nevada, and Texas) prohibit "sodomy" only between homosexuals. The name comes from the city of Sodom, destroyed by fire and brimstone in Genesis 19 because its male inhabitants attempt to "know" the two angels spending a night at Lot's house. Lot's sense of hospitality will not allow this; his sense of parental concern may be guessed from the fact that, as a consolation prize to the mob, he offers his two virgin daughters.

Spartan

We speak of austerity and toughness as *Spartan* qualities because the ancient Spartans ran a society that makes the U.S. Marines look like sissies. In the seventh century B.C., they adopted a code of laws that stressed hardiness and devotion to the state. The arts, considered enfeebling, were banished; sickly infants were left to die of exposure; military training started at age seven. It sounds fanatic, but it was also essential. Sparta had to be on constant alert because the daily work of the society was performed by a submerged class of *helots,* or serfs, who were constantly threatening rebellion.

Stoic

The Stoics were a group of philosophers, strongly influenced by the CYNICS, who held that the good life consisted of submission to the laws of the cosmos and a rational indifference to misfortune; thus *stoic* for "philosophically" calm or impassive. The founder of this very important school was Zeno of Citium (ca. 336–261 B.C.); his followers became known as Stoics because they met in the Athenian marketplace at the *Stoa Poikilē,* or Painted Portico.

Thug

Thug, for a brutal gangster or killer, derives from the Indian cult of Thuggee, whose members performed ritual murders in honor of the goddess Kali. Victims were strangled with scarves, their bodies mutilated before burial, and their possessions divided among cult members. The Thugs terrorized travelers in India for at least 600 years until they were eliminated by the British in the middle of the nineteenth century.

Titanic

The Titans in Greek mythology were the enormous, and enormously powerful, children of Uranus and Gaia (Heaven and Earth).

Chief among them was Cronus, who castrated and overthrew his father and was in turn overthrown, after a long and bitter struggle, by *his* son, Zeus—the sky god whom the Greeks, in a curious denial of genealogy, did not consider a Titan. Among the Titans who lent names to our language were Prometheus, ATLAS, and OCEAN.

Vandal

A wilful destroyer of property is called a *vandal* after the Germanic tribe of Vandals, who invaded and dominated the western Mediterranean in the fifth century A.D. Under their ambitious king Genseric, an army of 80,000 Vandals recklessly plundered Rome in 455; hence their unsavory reputation. Genseric also founded a North African kingdom which survived until 534.

Yahoo

Jonathan Swift's misanthropy is never displayed more caustically than in the fourth book of *Gulliver's Travels,* where Gulliver encounters a race of wise and benevolent horses, the Houyhnhnms, and a markedly inferior race of SLAVES, the coarse and imbecilic Yahoos. Because the Yahoos look suspiciously like Gulliver himself, the word immediately came to refer to any brutish or backward human being.

Yankee

This reference to New Englanders or, more broadly, northerners, goes back to a seventeenth-century epithet, "Jan Kees" or "Yankey," commonly applied to the Dutch by their maritime rivals the English: it seems to derive from Dutch *Janke,* the diminutive form of John. There also are tales of a Dutch pirate, or privateer, named Yankey, but these cannot be confirmed.

Zealot

First-century Jewish fundamentalists, the Zealots linked obedience to God's law with opposition to Roman control. Their use of ASSASSINATION and other violence gave *zealotry* a fanatical connotation, and that connotation showed its tragic light in the Zealots' defence of Masada. In 73 A.D., three years after Rome razed Jerusalem, nearly a thousand members of the sect still held out in this desert fortress; when their defeat became imminent, they committed mass suicide rather than surrender.

On the trail of apparent namesakes, you inevitably follow signs that lead nowhere. The TOM and JOHN sections of this book, for example, contain several ostensible eponyms that, upon closer inspection, admit of no personal referents. Herewith some additional cul-de-sacs.

Blanket

A tradition from Bristol, England, claims that native son Thomas Blanket was the originator of the product and the name in the middle of the fourteenth century. There is no sound evidence for this, since the French term *blanquette* (literally, "little white thing") was being used to describe undyed woolen cloth as early as 1300. The *Oxford English Dictionary* suggests, sensibly enough, that even if Thomas existed, he probably "took his name from the article," rather than the other way around.

Cesarean Section

The cesarean section, or C-section, was not, as is commonly believed, named after Julius Caesar. Legend connects it to him because he is thought to have been delivered abdominally, but the legend is misleading. In fact *cesarean* comes from the ancient *lex caesarea,* or "law of incision," which specified abdominal delivery when the mother had died close to term. Since Caesar's mother survived his birth, it is not likely he came into the world in this way.

Charley Horse

A *charley* in nineteenth-century England was a night watchman, the name thought to have been derived from that of Charles I, who expanded the London night watch. Some have made the leap from this to *charley* as a slang term for policeman, thence to *charley horse* for muscular stiffness, because such stiffness might arise from "riding Charley's horse," that is, walking a policeman's beat. Ingenious, but unsupported. The first appearance of the term is in 1889, in a Cincinnati, Ohio, paper, where it refers to a ball player's condition. H. L. Mencken, in his *The American Language,* suggests the player may have been Charles Esper, an obscure pitcher who "walked like a lame horse." Hendrickson surmises, not very enthusiastically, that it may refer to a horse named Charley that pulled the infield turf roller in Chicago just before the turn of the century.

Gadget

The World Almanac Book of Inventions gives a derivation of this word that I do so want to believe: it's a contraction of Gaget, Gauhier, & Cie., the construction firm that in 1886 built the Statue of Liberty; they sold miniature statues at the inauguration, instantly dubbed *gagets*. Unfortunately for this patriotic plum, *gadget* first entered English around 1855, to describe a "mechanical contrivance" (French *gâchette* means "lock tumbler"). But the first *printed* mention is guess when: 1886 on the button. Even desperate hope springs eternal.

Gaga

Willard Espy, citing Alfred Holt's *Word and Phrase Origins,* connects *gaga* hopefully to Paul Gauguin, because critics have seen his work as demented and because "the tongue slips easily" from the Impressionist to the expression. Pretty enough, but no evidence. Eric Partridge gives the origin as *gâteux,* French slang for a "feeble-minded oldster," but also admits (quite sensibly) that the term may have been influenced "by the echo of idiotic laughter." The Impressionist link would work better if the construction were *van gaga*.

Hooker

It is often said that this slang term for prostitute was coined by Civil War soldiers stationed in Washington, D.C., as poetic revenge on their commander, Union general Joseph Hooker, for putting the red-light district off limits. Hooker's biographers do not mention this, however, and the derivation is further confounded because the term first appears in America sometime in the 1850s—a decade before Fighting Joe Hooker was put on the capital watch. The most likely link is to the Hook, a New York City waterfront neighborhood that was notorious, from early in the nineteenth century, for the usual waterfront vices.

Jerry-Built

In an attempt to track down the original Jerry of this synonym for "cheaply constructed," the editors of the *Oxford English Dictionary* investigated a Lancashire building firm supposed to be notorious for shoddy work. They came up dry, leaving the origin open to conjecture. Brewer's *Dictionary of Phrase and Fable* offers two reasonable possibilities: that *jerry* is a short form of "Jericho," whose walls came tumbling down; and that it is a variant of "jury," from the use of "jury rigging" in emergencies. The eighteenth-century antiquarian Frances Grose brightly observes that "jury" in this sense may come from the French *journière*, "for the day" (only).

Tin Lizzie

Eric Partridge says that British seamen in World War I referred to H.M.S. *Queen Elizabeth* as a *tin Lizzie,* but the American referent is less clear. Commonly the term means a cheap automobile, especially the old Model T, which made Henry Ford a rich man in the early days of this century. Speculation as to the identity of Ford's Lizzie proves fruitless; the word is most likely a contraction for "limousine."

Mammon

Because of Jesus' observation in the Sermon on the Mount that "you cannot serve God and mammon," mammon is sometimes lumped together with Jehovah's Old Testament rivals—pagan gods like the Canaanite Baal and the PHILISTINES' Dagon—and assumed to be an actual person; the *Oxford English Dictionary* even says that medieval writers took the term as "the proper name of the devil of covetousness." This personification was after the fact. In Jesus' time, *mammon* was simply the Aramaic word for "riches."

Name Is Mud

If your name is mud, you are everyone's pariah. The expression is often said to refer to a Dr. Samuel Mudd, who set John Wilkes Booth's broken leg after his escape from Ford's Theater and was imprisoned for complicity after the fact. Appropriate but untrue. In fact the phrase *name is mud* was common in England by the early 1820s, a decade and a half before Booth was born.

Palooka

This derogatory term for a third-rate boxer sounds as if it comes from Joe Palooka, the good-hearted, naive hero of Ham Fisher's syndicated comic strip. The strip began in 1928, however, and Mitford Mathews discovered the word in print a good three years before that—so it is likely that battling Joe was named for the generic, not vice versa. H. L. Mencken calls it originally a racetrack gibe, indicating a "sorry nag."

Round-Robin

A *round-robin,* used first by mutinous sailors, is a protest or petition signed by several parties, with the signatures appearing in a circle to conceal which person signed first. (John HANCOCK would have abhorred it.) WEBSTER suggests the term is linked to the proper name Robin, but does not say which one. A plausible alternative is offered by the good doctor Brewer, who takes it as a corruption of the French *rond ruban,* or "round ribbon." Perhaps the original round-robins were secured with ribbons; perhaps the signatures themselves resembled a ribbon of names.

Jolly Roger

The macabre humor of outlawry is nowhere better exemplified than in the eighteenth-century pirates' name for their standard, the skull-and-crossbones on a black background widely known as the *Jolly Roger. Jolly* may have been suggested by the ostensible grin of the death's head, but nobody really knows where the seagoing THUGS got *Roger.* Partridge gives the original usage as "old Roger," which doesn't make things any clearer. A long-forgotten Blackbeard, perhaps, or the ghost of the hanged Captain Kidd.

Sirloin

Among amateur etymologists a favorite chestnut is an anecdote about the word "sirloin" being the result of a royal joke. According to the story, a British king—variously identified as Henry VIII, James I, or Charles II—was so pleased with a certain cut of beef that he knighted it "Sir Loin" on the spot. A charming tale, but untrue. The actual derivation is from the French *sur longe,* or "above the loin"—indicating that part of the animal from which the sirloin is taken.

Terry Cloth

The common beach-towel material was neither invented nor popularized by a Terry. The origin of the term is uncertain, but WEBSTER and the *Oxford English Dictionary* agree that *terry* is probably a form of the French *tirer,* meaning "to pull" or "to draw." Terry cloth, a pile fabric, is woven with a double set of warp and weft, one set forming a ground and the other being drawn through this ground to create the fabric's characteristic loops.

Bibliography

Inevitably, the research for most of the entries in this book began with that logophile's bible, the *Oxford English Dictionary. I* am also indebted to the standard British, American, and continental encyclopedias and biographical dictionaries; to the various books cited in the text; and to the following specialized sources. I have starred those volumes that were particularly provocative or helpful.

Avery, Catherine, ed. *The New Century Classical Handbook.* Appleton Century Crofts, 1962.

*Benét, William Rose. *The Reader's Encyclopedia.* Harper & Row, 1965.

Brewer, E. C. *Brewer's Dictionary of Phrase and Fable.* Revised edition by Ivor H. Evans. Harper & Row, 1981.

*Espy, Willard R. *O Thou Improper, Thou Uncommon Noun.* Clarkson Potter, 1978.

Ewing, W. and J.E.H. Thomson. *Temple Dictionary of the Bible.* J. M. Dent, 1910.

Funk, Wilfred. *Word Origins and Their Romantic Stories.* Bell Publishing, 1978.

Funke, Charles Earle. *Thereby Hangs a Tale: Stories of Curious Word Origins.* Harper & Brothers, 1950.

Grose, Frances. *Dictionary of the Vulgar Tongue* (1785; 1811). Follett Publishing, 1971.

Harper's Bible Dictionary. Paul J. Achtemeier, general editor. Harper & Row, 1985.

*Hendrickson, Robert. *The Dictionary of Eponyms: Names That Became Words*. Stein & Day, 1985.

Hunt, Cecil. *Word Origins: The Romance of Language*. Philosophical Library, 1962.

*Mathews, Mitford, ed. *A Dictionary of Americanisms on Historical Principles*. University of Chicago Press, 1951.

Morris, William and Mary Morris. *Dictionary of Word and Phrase Origins*. 2 vols. Harper & Row, 1962 and 1967.

*Partridge, Eric. *A Dictionary of Slang and Unconventional English*. Eighth edition by Paul Beale. Macmillan, 1984.

Shipley, Joseph T. *Dictionary of Word Origins*. Littlefield, Adams & Company, 1961.

Stapleton, Michael. *A Dictionary of Greek and Roman Mythology*. Bell Publishing, 1978.

Index

Index

Index